P9-DHJ-283

THE DO-IT-YOURSELF
PSYCHOTHERAPY BOOK

Other books by Martin Shepard

The Love Treatment
A Psychiatrist's Head
Fritz
Beyond Sex Therapy
Someone You Love Is Dying

and, with Marjorie Lee:

Games Analysts Play
Marathon 16
Sexual Marathon

The Do-It-Yourself Psychotherapy Book

by Martin Shepard, M.D.

E. P. Dutton & Co., Inc.   New York

The book *Awareness: Exploring, Experimenting,
Experiencing* by John O. Stevens is copyright © 1971
by John O. Stevens. The quotation on page 20 is reprinted
by permission of Real People Press.

This paperback edition of
The Do-It-Yourself Psychotherapy Book
first published 1976 by E. P. Dutton & Co., Inc.
Copyright © 1973 by Martin Shepard, M.D.
All rights reserved. Printed in the U.S.A.

10 9 8 7 6 5 4 3 2 1

No part of this publication may be reproduced or
transmitted in any form or by any means, electronic or
mechanical, including photocopy, recording, or any
information storage and retrieval system now known or to
be invented, without permission in writing from the
publisher, except by a reviewer who wishes to quote brief
passages in connection with a review written for inclusion
in a magazine, newspaper or broadcast.

Published simultaneously in Canada by Clarke, Irwin &
Company Limited, Toronto and Vancouver

ISBN 0-8415-0447-4
Library of Congress Catalog Card Number: 76-11881

to Judy

THIS book was written both for "normal" people interested in living an even richer and more fulfilling existence and for those individuals who feel themselves to be "neurotic," troubled, adrift, or otherwise unhappy.

For this second group, the *Do-It-Yourself* approach is presented as a very real *alternative* to formal psychotherapy. Followed conscientiously, it should enrich the lives of many who attempt it. Yet, just as no single school of psychotherapy can legitimately claim to be a universal "cure-all," neither does the Do-It-Yourself system.

Those who do the work outlined in the following pages and find no improvement in their lives can always consider the possibilities of seeing a professional therapist. Such help —in the form of Encounter Groups or formal psychotherapy (and involving the time and costs that they do)—seems warranted, to me, only after attempting a self-directed approach.

There is an ancient medical dictum which requires that the simplest therapies be tried before implementing more complex and laborious ones. It is in accordance with that principle that this book is offered.

MARTIN SHEPARD, M.D.

CONTENTS

1

HONESTY AND COUNTERPHOBIA

IT is clear that many of us pass too much of our lives living in a state of conflict, and too little of our time living naturally —*living in accordance with our own natures.* The reasons for this are equally clear to any student of psychology. We have been raised to feel it is "wrong" to express various facets of our personality. How "wrong" we feel it is to express either tenderness, lust, anger, need, or independence—alone or in combination—determines our degree of so-called mental health or mental illness.

When we believe that certain parts of our "being" are bad, *we suffer from failing to satisfy these distrusted needs and impulses.* Like the adolescent schoolboy who is reluctant to approach the girl he cares about for fear she will find his desire for her "offensive," we may remain distant, secret, and lonely admirers. Or, *we suffer from crippling symptoms designed to mask our "bad" impulses.* We can develop tics to disguise our anger, ulcers to hide our competitiveness, phobias to stifle our urges for independence. And when these normal impulses do break out—despite our very best efforts to control them—they break out with a power and a force a hundred times greater than usual. It is like water bursting from behind a dam. It will have a catastrophic effect on the valley below. Yet it isn't the water itself that is responsible. Rather, it is the damming-up process that invites the holocaust.

For some thirty years now, people living in Western civilizations have turned to psychotherapists when they wished to abandon their self-conflicts and live in greater self-harmony. This process of going from "illness" to "health" is termed *psychotherapy*. It is my contention, after more than ten years of clinical practice, that most troubled individuals can make this transition without spending—or, in many cases, *wasting* —their money on a therapist. The purpose of this book is to provide you with a psychological road map so that you might arrive at your destination most directly, most rapidly, and at the lowest possible fare.

All the formal psychotherapies—be they the various schools of psychoanalysis (Freudian, Adlerian, Kleinian, Jungian, Sullivanian, Rogerian) or the other popular psychotherapies (Gestalt, Transactional Analysis, Psychodrama, Rational-Emotive Therapy, Group Therapy, or Encounter Groups)— share two themes. One element common to all these systems is that one person (the patient) tells another person (the therapist) or a group of people what is honestly on his or her mind. Through this process, "shameful" material (angry, sexual, or dependent feelings and/or activities, self-indulgences, deceits, etc.) is eventually shared. The therapist (or the group) accepts the patient notwithstanding these "bad" thoughts, feelings, and acts. Through the acceptance of this other human or group of humans, the patient finds self-acceptance.

In addition, to one degree or another, the "patient" is encouraged to act against his fears and break his repetitive, self-defeating patterns. This is done directly in Encounter

Groups, Rational-Emotive Therapy, and Psychodrama and indirectly in the various forms of psychoanalysis, Transactional Analysis, and Gestalt Therapy. The indirect approach consists of the supposedly nondirective therapist asking questions ("Have you ever thought of . . . ?" "Why haven't you . . . ?") or directing his interest, analysis, and attention to areas where the person seems to be on an emotional treadmill. Either way, the patient is encouraged to dare to be himself and be less dependent on the opinions and regard of others.

In effect, then, successful psychotherapy changes a shame-ridden, closed-in person into a shameless and open one. And it does so by the twin processes of asking for honest, open expression of oneself to other people *and* by requesting one to act counterphobically (against one's fears). These are the twin pillars that this book is based upon.

"How do I know I can do it on my own?" you might well ask. You don't. But there is no assurance that you will better your condition by seeing a psychotherapist either. Critics of psychotherapy are quick to point to studies that indicate that prospective patients on a psychiatric clinic's waiting list do as well, statistically, as those patients seen by the resident therapists. Or the same critics will mock the entire field of psychotherapy by singling out other studies showing that 33⅓ percent of people who see therapists improve, 33⅓ percent remain about the same, and 33⅓ percent show a worsening of symptoms.

Still, any clinician will tell you that those people who do improve are the ones who both dare to be open and honest *and* dare to act against their fears. It seems, then, that the achievement of a harmonious, self-accepting state depends more on the motivation of the individual patient than it does on the skill of the individual therapist. So your chances of improving on a Do-It-Yourself approach depend in large part (as they would if you were to see a therapist) on what you put into it. Besides which, you are not really "doing-it-on-your-own." For in this approach you will still have to share your thoughts, desires, and actions with other people. Except that they will be lay people, and not therapists.

"But ordinary people aren't properly trained," you might counter. "They aren't as stable. They may react the wrong way. They may disapprove of what I tell them or offer confusing suggestions." Here, too, all I can tell you is that you are correct. Lay people may do that. But so may therapists. For therapists are human too. They are laymen with a little formal training in the field of psychology. They have feelings, prejudices, values, that they often try—with only varying degrees of success—to hide. Indeed, one may well question the stability of psychotherapists in general, who, more often than not, first gravitated toward their field because of their own personal problems. Or the stability of psychiatrists in particular, for this profession has a suicide rate higher than that in any other subspecialty in the field of medicine.

Actually there are some distinct advantages in revealing yourself to an "ordinary person" instead of a therapist. If, for instance, a lay person reacts "untherapeutically," you can pick yourself up, dust yourself off, and try again. If a therapist reacts the same way, you immediately presume it to be "your fault." It hurts more and you are less likely to attempt the same revelations. Similarly, if a therapist reacts with acceptance, you are never sure whether this is because he is being paid by you or was trained to *act* this way. Neither factor beclouds the acceptance that comes from your peers.

Another disadvantage of revealing yourself to a therapist (as opposed to a layman) is that it reinforces your erroneous feeling that there is really something wrong with you; that, to use Thomas Harris' phrase, you're "Not-OK."* Basically, everyone is all right. Yet, as Harris has ably put it, we all grow up feeling (to one degree or another) that we're Not-OK. The Not-OK idea is a natural result of childhood—even a good one—what with the hundreds of thousands of admonitions all children must hear in the course of their childhoods. This leads the child (vis-à-vis the parent) to the "I'm Not-OK–You Are" position, and bespeaks a derogation of self and elevation of other. He may settle for this maladjustment or overcompensate by choosing a new one ("I'm OK—It's you who are Not-OK").

Obviously the "I'm OK—You're OK" position is the only one in life that can truly satisfy. Yet by seeing a "therapist" (an OK expert who deals with Not-OK people), we reinforce the "I'm Not-OK–You Are" bind. And many therapists, being trained to deal with "pathology," seem to sniff out and continuously remind their patients of their Not-OKness. When two adolescents share the fact that they masturbate with one another, they both leave feeling, "I'm OK." When you tell a poker-faced therapist about the same activity, you're likely to feel Not-OK.

Despite these criticisms, I do not wish to damn the traditional psychotherapies or any individual therapist. It is true that many therapists become so immersed in their theories, so religious about their particular sect's approach, that they further confuse and mislead their lost clients. Others, however, have consistently challenged and encouraged their patients to be honest and risk acting on their insights and feelings. What I do wish to do is to impress the reader with *what he or she must do in order to change.* And *do* something, he must.

All of our psychotherapies are heavily influenced by psycho-

* See *I'm OK—You're OK* by Thomas A. Harris (New York, Harper & Row, 1969).

analytic thinking. Two popular fallacies that have resulted from this are "the myth of the big secret" and that "the past is the major determinant of the present." The popular treatment of analysis in books, films, and articles has caused many people to expect that their lives will change when they only discover that one, big, repressed trauma that happened in their childhoods. This is the "myth of the big secret," for, aside from one or two of Freud's earliest cases and isolated rare instances between, such insight alone does not cure (if any such secret ever existed in the first place).

The second psychoanalytic aberration is, unfortunately, perpetuated by many of its practitioners. They are so aware of the past's influence on current behavior that they encourage their patients to reminisce about the past continuously and pay scant attention to encouraging modification of present behavior. For while it is true that we are affected by our past, it is equally true that *our present of today is the past of tomorrow*. Thus, by working on the present, we can make our tomorrows significantly brighter.

The Do-It-Yourself approach is intended especially for those people who are tired of the vagaries of traditional therapies, who realize that change comes from action, and who prefer change to buying a therapist's shoulder to cry on.

Instead of the free-association approach that occurs on an analyst's couch, the Do-It-Yourself method will focus, chapter by chapter, on those particular areas of life that cause many of us complications. Various tasks (actions, exercises) will be suggested at the end of each chapter which, if performed, should help you to act against your fears and lead to a more honest, open, and self-accepting existence.

The Transactional Analysts (Eric Berne, in *Games People Play*, and Thomas Harris, in *I'm OK—You're OK*) attempt, in their therapeutic approach, to strengthen the Adult in each of us, while at the same time appreciating our Child part and our internalized Parent. The Adult is the part that senses what you want, displays dispassion, serves to consummate your desires, is open to discovery, and is *unashamed.* These aims are also the aims of the Do-It-Yourself system.

One final advantage of the Do-It-Yourself method, of course, is that it does not cost you anything other than your own efforts. Many people currently in therapy could possibly save their $25–$100-per-week psychotherapeutic bills, buy some new clothes, take that vacation they've always wanted, or otherwise pamper themselves with their newfound savings.

What I will stress, continuously, is *honesty* and *action.* That *deeds* are as important as *words* in attaining a state of psychological health is an idea whose time has come. The new wave of Growth Centers (Anthos, Esalen, Oasis, Quest, and many, many more) and their popularity with the public have already proven that fact. Many of the exercises you will be asked to perform were developed and proven effective in these same centers.

Many of these tasks involve risk-taking. You can tell when you approach a risk because of the gnawing feeling in your belly. This is called "anxiety." If you work with anxiety properly you will soon learn to welcome rather than fear it. For it means that you have a chance to do something "different"— that you have an opportunity to expand your personal boundaries—that you are about to enter the process of countering your phobias.

Just as in traditional psychotherapy, each individual will determine his own growth and rate of change. You are as free to reject the exercises as you are to perform them. Do what makes sense to you. And accept responsibility for what you choose to do or not do. For I accept none of it for you.

This book should be read slowly. You ought to allot yourself a week or two to complete each chapter. Along the way you will, I hope, have some good experiences, joyful adventures, and gain new awareness and greater self-acceptance in the process.

2

SECRETS

IF the way to "mental health" is based upon *honesty* and *action*, it is fitting to begin the Do-It-Yourself method by proposing a series of activities designed to help you become aware of and eliminate your present deceptions. For no man or woman can ever hope to find self-contentment until that person is *content* to be truly and simply him or herself. Without artifice and without deception. That means you will have to give up (should you have any) your most obvious lies and, most important, expose your secrets.

Secrets come in all sizes, shapes, ways, and forms. We are told something by a friend and asked to "keep it a secret." We have certain things about ourselves that we would never tell anybody. And we have opinions regarding others that we would be most reluctant to share.

Secrets, as I see them, are a form of lie and, for the most part, quite damaging to the individual who has them. Whereas most people are motivated to give up their lies (we tend to dislike outright falseness both in ourselves and others), secrets are often seen as "necessary" or "decent" acts. We hold something back about ourselves because we feel it is "base," "awful," or "unlovable." At other times we keep a secret "for the other person's sake," because "he couldn't take it," because telling someone what you truly feel (assuming it is unflattering) would be "unkind." Whereas *lies* are black, *secrets* are white. In actuality, secrets are simply lies of *omission*.

Many people defend their keeping of secrets with the cliché "What he doesn't know won't hurt him." This is true. What the secret-keeper fails to appreciate is how he hurts himself in the process.

There are many ways in which secrets oppress the secret-holder. All personal secrets (things I would not want someone else to know about me) invariably touch on some aspect of shame or guilt. When you finally decide to share these with someone else, there is usually an immediate feeling of relief. If your secret is then acceptingly received by the person it is told to, you feel cleansed, refreshed, and able to continue your life free of the burdens of shame and guilt that resulted in the secret's being kept for so long. It is as though a great weight had been put down. The time, energy, and concentration which previously had been devoted to keeping your story hidden are now no longer necessary and are available, instead, for creative work.

I can recall three rather dramatic instances of people's lives being changed for the better for having revealed their secrets. One concerned a woman in her late thirties—let us call her Jane—who secretly resented the attention her husband lavished on his family (parents, brothers, and sisters) to the exclusion of her and their children. She was ashamed of her feelings, for she herself was raised to believe that strong family ties were a good thing, that resentfulness was a bad thing, and that a "good wife's role was to make her husband happy." Still, the resentfulness simmered inside her daily, particularly since her husband worked in a family business and was involved with these people not only socially but professionally.

Jane developed symptoms to both mask and express her dissatisfaction. She began to have anxiety attacks that indirectly required her husband to pay more attention to her. She couldn't cope with her housework. One day, while serving a Sunday dinner to her husband's family, she burned everything, began shaking, started talking hysterically, and "ruined" everybody's good time.

Her husband had responded to all this with consideration at first, but then with mounting irritation at her for pulling him away from his work and relatives—particularly since his initial reassurances seemed to do no good. Jane responded apologetically and tearfully, properly assumed all of the blame, and added that she felt she was having a "breakdown." The day that she cooked (and burned) the relatives' dinner was the night that she entered a psychiatric hospital.

The first few weeks in the hospital helped her not one iota. She was still attempting to live up to her image as "the good wife" and tried, therefore, to control her symptoms and resentfulness with medication. Only the drugs didn't work. And her husband complained of the expense.

One weekend, while at home on a pass, she "broke." Her husband had apparently gone too far. He threatened to leave her if she couldn't control herself. "Who cares," she finally said in utter despair. "You were never with me anyway." She went on to express all the secret resentments and grudges she harbored for being neglected, and in addition told her husband that he could damn well leave any time he felt like it.

She returned to the hospital that Sunday night beaming. Her nervousness was gone. Her husband was shocked and surprised. He had never known how she felt about his family and decided, shortly afterward, that if he had to choose between Jane and his relatives, he easily preferred Jane.

Another instance concerned a professional man who had been in a state of depression for ten years following the death of his wife in an automobile crash. Although previously an outgoing sort of person, he had kept very much to himself since that time. He had seen analysts and attended groups, but nothing seemed to help.

One weekend he came to a risk-taking Encounter Group hoping, he felt, to share some good feelings with other people. At one point, someone proposed that everyone tell his biggest secret. Everyone had a go at it except this man, whom I'll call Ben.

"I'm not ready yet," he said when his turn came.

The next day, summoning up all of his courage, he decided, finally, to risk telling the secret he had kept these ten years (a secret he had even kept from his previous analyst). I suppose he was encouraged by the good responses other people were having from having unburdened themselves of their secrets.

"I killed my wife," he said, his face a contorted mask. And then he burst out crying.

It was a most emotion-filled hour that followed. He talked some more and people asked questions. It turned out that he had been very unhappily married yet, being a Catholic, felt unable to ask for a divorce. His wife was an alcoholic. One night, while both were drinking in a bar, she—by far the more drunk of the two—decided she wanted to drive home.

"I know I should have stopped her from driving," he said. "But I also knew how relieved I would be if she killed herself in a crash."

They got in the car together and, while driving back, he reached over and put his hand on the wheel. The car went into a tree. Ben lived. His wife died.

It wasn't clear after this confession (nor was it, most likely, at the time) whether Ben grabbed the wheel in an unsuccessful attempt to avoid the crash, or whether he hoped to kill the two of them. What was certain was that this was no cold-blooded murder attempt. Just because he wished her dead was no reason to assume he killed her.

The people he told his secret to were quite moved by his plight. Clearly he had suffered enough. He was accepted, held, reassured, respected. His crying gave way to his first happiness in a decade. He had put his burden down, no longer had to remain distant and guarded with his fellows, and left the weekend hoping to live a more satisfying existence.

My third illustration concerns a young lesbian, Grace, who was hospitalized after several suicide attempts. Her greatest source of concern was that her mother might discover that she—Grace—was a lesbian. This was her big secret, and to keep it she had to go through elaborate excuses, rationalizations, and invent numerous cover stories to hide her activities from Momma.

When Momma visited the hospital, she, Grace, and the psychiatrist sat down for a three-way chat. To Grace's chagrin, the psychiatrist told Momma Grace's secret. To Grace's surprise, Momma was accepting of her daughter's sexuality. Her attitude might be summed up by her saying, in effect, "As long as Grace goes out with a nice Jewish girl . . ."

Here again, a depression lifted, elaborate disguises could be abandoned, and Grace could live a more guilt-free life. Jane, Ben, and Grace all illustrate how, when a personal secret is out in the open, shame disappears and living becomes easier. It is no longer necessary to act furtively, secretly, and peculiarly to keep the truth from others' eyes.

When a patient comes into a therapist's office, he usually

feels ashamed of certain feelings and activities which he therefore hides from other people. He feels that these feelings and
activities are what make him neurotic. If he has a successful
course of therapy he begins to realize that what is neurotic are
not these feelings and actions but rather the *defensive dodges
and furtive maneuverings he uses to hide these invariably quite
human responses from other people.*

Many experts have described "neurosis" and "psychosis"
in terms of communication difficulties. Messages aren't given
or received clearly by people with "mental illness." Of course
not. No one can communicate clearly if he has lots of things
he wishes to hide. And the more you hide—the more difficulty you have in communication—the "sicker" you are considered to be.

There are other ways, too, in which secrets harm you. I
am thinking particularly of secrets kept "for someone else's
sake." Closer examination usually reveals it to be your own
skin that you *think* you are protecting.

For years a mouthwash manufacturer successfully sold his
product behind the slogan "Even your best friend won't tell
you." People bought the mouthwash for they themselves knew
that they would never tell a person if he or she had bad breath.
Therefore it was conceivable they had it and nobody told
them.

I would suggest that when we fail to tell a person he has
bad breath we are not "doing it for his sake." For if he knew
the problem, he might solve it. Rather, we hold back, like the
messenger who fears to deliver bad news to the king. The
messenger is aware that as the harbinger of ill tidings, he will
be punished. So do we fear, in some primitive way, of carrying
"bad news" to people.

We tend not to tell people if they are ill mannered or offend
us. We say we hold back "for their sake." Yet I believe we

hold back for fear of their retaliation, thinking that they would act like the ancient kings who scapegoated messengers, *or* for fear of showing our vulnerability—showing that things *do* bother us; that we are not the super-cool people that we pretend to be. In practicing these petty deceptions, however, we deny the other person the opportunity to change and we deny revealing ourselves *as we really are*.

I have seen patients with terminal illnesses who ask their doctors or family what is wrong. Invariably those who are told the truth *when they ask* fare better than those who are lied to. For at some point in their illnesses, all know that they are going to die. You can't keep that a secret from a dying man forever. All that can result from such withholding is that now the dying person will feel deceived by those he trusts and unable to discuss and share his considerable feelings about passing from this existence. Here again, the supposed purpose of such secrets is "to spare one." Nonsense. It is our not being able or willing to share such news that causes the deception.

Of all the secrets kept "for the other person's sake," the most prevalent, probably, concerns infidelity. I have had many people come into my office and tell me of some secret affair that they are having.

"Does your spouse know about it?" I will usually ask.

"No," is the typical reply. "She couldn't take it." Or, "It would hurt him too much if he found out."

Often I will see husbands and wives separately. It is not uncommon for both to be secretly cheating on one another. Each assumes the other is faithful and would be hurt if he found out. Each feels somewhat guilty about his affair. Both would welcome it if their supposedly "devoted" spouse had some peccadillo—for then they could carry on in a guilt-free way—but neither will be the first to confess his secret.

When you get past the benevolent explanation of the secret,

however, you usually find that the secret-holder is trying to protect him or herself. He doesn't want to give up his affair nor does he want to be abandoned by a hurt, jealous, or resentful spouse. By keeping a secret each avoids confrontations, but no longer do they have an open, honest relationship with one another.

What would happen if they kept no secrets? One of three things, I suppose. Either their spouse would accept such activity (and many currently do), or would leave them (and they perhaps would find someone who loved and accepted them as they are), or they would be asked to choose between lover and mate. It is, more often than not, that last possibility that our secret-keeper wishes to avoid. He wants to have his cake and eat it too. Yet, if the choice is that difficult, what does it say about the nature of the marital relationship?

Many times people profess to keep their affairs a secret because exposure would be "cruel" to their husbands or wives. A bigger secret that they keep is that they no longer *love* their spouses. In the attempt to be "uncruel" many a husband will hide his lack of love for many years, only to have his wife discover it when she is in her mid-forties and less likely to make a new life for herself. Or I think of another instance of a woman, Alice (a pseudonym, as are the other examples used in this book), who did not "have the heart" to tell her husband that she didn't love him. She remained unresponsive sexually and tended to criticize him a lot, so as to keep him at bay physically. By continuing to live with him she prevented herself from finding greater happiness with another man. Her husband, unaware of her secret, tried to figure out again and again what he was doing wrong, so as to please her. Of course, since she didn't love him, nothing worked.

Many of these types of supposedly "kindhearted" secrets do, in fact, perpetrate both minor and major cruelties on those we live with. For they deprive our partners of making enlightened choices by keeping our own agendas hidden. This is still another way in which secrets hurt the secret-keeper. Because he knows that his secret is cruel, that it is harmful, that it is dishonest. And we cannot really appreciate and love ourselves when we are engaged in such practices.

These self-damaging aspects of keeping secrets lead me to postulate a basic rule for self-acceptance, shameless living, and mental health:

Don't do anything you can't share, and be prepared to discuss everything that you do.

There is still a further way in which secrets harm you. For they may keep you from getting what you want. I am thinking here of the shy man or woman who is reluctant to profess his attraction or love for another person, and so keeps it a secret. Often the other person is unaware of the shy one's feelings, or is equally shy. Therefore nothing develops. If, on the other hand, the secret desire were shared, a possibility would exist for its fruition.

I recall a man who was unsatisfied with his wife sexually. A decent man, he was reluctant to "criticize" her. Instead, he began masturbating daily to relieve his sexual tensions but kept it a secret from his wife as he felt it "unseemly." When, in an Encounter group, he did share his secret, his wife, who cared for him very much, began to examine her own behavior to see what she might do to please him more.

How many women have kept the secret that they don't have orgasms with their husbands or lovers? Their reasons? They are either "afraid of offending the male ego," or ashamed of their unresponsiveness. So they fake it. But by keeping it a secret they never truly satisfy themselves. Were they to share their secret, it is quite conceivable that a tender, considerate, and skillful mate would respond to them with sufficient care and devotion so as to assure their being able to climax.

So far I've talked about the benefits to be obtained through abandoning secrets. What about the harmful effects? you might ask. I am sure that there are some, yet I can honestly say that I have never seen any long-term damage done from being honest. Quite the contrary. The advantages surely seem to outweigh those of the secretive approach. While it is true that deciding to be honest may, at first, cause you certain *incon-veniences*, it rarely produces the *catastrophes* you might envisage. Friends and relations do not usually huff and puff and walk away when you are truthful. Some might, of course. A "friend" may shun you, a spouse leave, a boss fire you. But then you must wonder how solid and respectful the relation-ship was in the first place.

With all these arguments to be made against keeping secrets, why, one asks, did we develop them in the first place? The answer harks back, of course, to childhood. We all want love. We all start to feel Not-OK as children. We try to hide our Not-OKness so as to insure our parents' loving us. Thus we keep secret that which our parents told us was "unlovable." It varies from family to family. One parent considers aggres-siveness lovable and passivity unlovable. To another the reverse is true. If Poppa and Momma disagree, we are in a real fix. A child cannot recognize this bind. A grown-up can. Since your world no longer consists of your father and mother, and not all your feelings and reactions will please everyone, your best course, it seems to me, is to be truly yourself at all times and trust that you will find someone who accepts and loves you *as you are* instead of qualifiedly accepting you because of *what you pretend to be*.

John Stevens, in his book *Awareness*, puts it as well as anyone:

A great deal has been written about trust and love, and that if you can build a trusting, loving relationship, then people can be honest with each other. I believe this idea is exactly backwards. It is very nice if I feel trusting and loving toward someone, but if I don't feel this way, what can I do about it? Trust and love are my *feeling responses* toward another person, and these responses cannot be manufactured. Either I feel love or I don't. All the emphasis on trust and love results in many people *pretending* to feel trust and love "because it is healthy, and will bring about closeness, honesty, etc."—adding a new area of phoniness and dishonesty in their behavior.

Honesty, however, is a *behavior* and *is* something I can choose or not choose. I cannot decide to love or trust, but I can decide to be personally honest or not. And when I choose to be really honest and say what I experience and what I feel, I am showing that I can be trusted. In order to do this I have to first be honest with myself and get in touch with my experiencing, and take responsibility for it by expressing it as my experiencing. This is the *only* kind of behavior that can bring about a response of trust. Trust is my response to a person that I know I can believe. Even if I dislike a person, I can trust him if he is honest with me, and I can respect his willingness to be himself honestly. When I trust and respect myself enough to be myself honestly, others respond with trust and respect.

Likewise, honesty does not always bring a response of love, but it is absolutely essential to it. When I am honestly myself, and you respond warmly and with caring, then love exists. If I calculate and put on phony behavior in order to please you, you may love my *behavior*, but you cannot love *me*, because I have hidden my real existence behind this artificial behavior. Even when you love in response to my phony behavior, I cannot really receive your love. It is poisoned by my knowledge that the love is for the image I have created, not for me. I also have to be continually on guard to be sure that I maintain my image so that your love does not disappear. Since I have shut myself off from your love in this way,

I will feel more lonely and unloved, and try even more desperately to manipulate myself and you in order to get this love. This is the tragic fallacy in all behavior that is based on fantasy and images, intention and manipulation. Whenever I manipulate myself in order to get a certain response from you, I know that your response is not directed toward *me*, so it gives me little satisfaction. All that effort to bring about a response that I can never really enjoy! In contrast, when I am honestly myself and you respond to me as I am in that moment, I can receive this fully and know the satisfaction of being really related with you. This honest relating is not always joyful or pleasant—it is sometimes sad, sometimes angry, etc.—but it is always *solid* and *real* and *vitally alive*.

A self-therapy program must begin, then, by asking you to discover yourself and lose your shame by giving up your secrets. This is, as well, the first opportunity you shall have to test your determination to overcome your fears—to test your counterphobic strength. The following exercises will ask you to reveal things you might fear will make you unaccept-able. So it is a big risk. Yet, if you are either desperate or adventurous enough, you will follow my suggestions and, I hope, come to feel the satisfactions of being acceptable as you truly are.

The exercises require no further explanation. They are presented to you as things to experience and think about *after* you have performed them.

EXERCISES

1. Think of the thoughts you are most ashamed of right now. Write them down. Pretend someone else has told you these things. What words would you have for that person? Give your counsel aloud.

2. Do the same thing with old shames of childhood, adolescence, and early adulthood.

3. Tell your closest friends (at least two people) of these things.

4. Tell a relative stranger (someone you work with, someone at a cocktail party) the same things.

5. Tell someone you like from a distance that you like him.

6. Tell your closest friend something that you admire about him or her that you've never shared before.

7. Tell this same friend of the thing you resent most about him.

8. Repeat exercises 6 and 7 with your lover.

9. Tell your spouse (girl friend, boy friend) that secret which, if shared, would most threaten your relationship.

10. Ask people you know to ask you the most personal, private question they dare—and try to answer them honestly.

11. Keep a small notebook in your pocket and jot down in it each and every evasion you practice in a single day—no matter how petty (i.e., telling people what you think they *want* to hear rather than what you truly feel). Study the list each night— both for cues as to what you are afraid of, and to see if you can gradually give up these deceptions.

12. Make a list of from five to ten specific exercises to work on the specific evasions you have caught yourself at in exercise 11. Include evasions of *omission* (what you *didn't* say but wanted to) as well as *commission* (spoken deceptions).

Allow yourself a minimum time of one week to work on these assignments before going on to the exercises of Chapter 3.

3

BLAME

AT this point I would like to raise the question as to whether you have engaged in any self-blame for not doing "well enough" in the exercises in Chapter 2. Are you berating yourself for having avoided certain ones? Are you chastising yourself for having performed "poorly" in those you did do? Or have other people had a bad reaction to your efforts? Do you blame me, perhaps, for suggesting such "impossible" exercises?

I ask these questions because *blame* is a game that I think you can do without. It frustrates. It usually adds insult to injury. It tends to cause conflicts and mutual recriminations. Most important, it prevents you from growing, keeps you guilt-ridden (in cases of self-blame), and prevents you from taking responsibility for your own life (when you blame others).

This chapter, then, will explore *blame* and offer various exercises designed to help you surmount this troubling and unnecessary emotion.

The first thing to understand when you are engaged in blaming behavior—of either self or others—is the total illogicality of blame. For wouldn't everyone do the *right* thing if he were free to choose? Wouldn't you have performed all twelve of the exercises and done them faultlessly? Wouldn't

I have written up these same procedures so as to help you stretch your "growing" muscles without overtaxing you? Of course we both would have. If things didn't work out perfectly, it is only because this is a very imperfect world. And we, as part of it, are also imperfect beings. That part of it can't be helped. It is part of the human condition. It deserves neither sorrow, blame, pity, nor praise. It just *is*.

If something doesn't work out the way you or I would like it to, disappointment is natural enough. Blaming yourself, however, only adds further unhappiness. You are already disappointed. Why add further aggravation in the form of self-blame?

And if you blame *me*—or some third party—for your disappointment, that will only get our hackles up. We are likely to throw the blame ball back to you since you've "not tried hard enough." This can go back and forth for many, many rounds. The result? We add hurt feelings, resentfulness, and, at times, unbridgeable antagonisms to our already disappointing disappointment.

Besides which, who says that you have to succeed immediately in any new undertaking? Disappointments and failures are necessary for growth, change, and the learning of new skills. For learning only grows out of *trial and failure*. If we can do something right the first time, then we haven't learned anything new. For we were capable of doing it all along. Often, in fact, we learn that we cannot do something only when we fail at it. At that point, persistence, trial and *error* (failure), going back to the drawing boards to figure out a new approach, and trying again in a *somewhat different manner* are the keys to eventual success. Along the way there are certain painful disappointments, but also personal growth. That is what is meant by the term growing pains.

Blame of other people usually occurs when they fail to live up to *your* expectations. But why should they? Would you be willing to live up to theirs? Do you want to live up to any-body's expectations other than your own? Don't other people have a right to do what *they* want to do instead of what *you* want them to do? Don't they have the same rights as you to be wrong, make mistakes, and, perhaps, learn and grow in the process?

Examples of blaming others for not living up to one's expectations are commonly seen in all relationships where people spend a significant part of their lives together. Parent/child and husband/wife combinations invariably contain a certain degree of this interaction.

Consider, if you will, the mother whose daughter moves away from home. She will blame her daughter for not phoning or visiting more regularly since this is her expectation of what "the ideal child" would do. The daughter, on the other hand, resents and blames her mother for subtly insisting that she pay more ritualistic attention to her. For daughter's expectation is that mother should be "the ideal mother." And ideal mothers let their children leave the home without trying to make them feel guilty.

One eleven-year-old that I know blames her mother for not being around to spend more time with her. Mother works three days a week and is not home to greet her children after school on those days. Neither is she able to serve them their meal, which she has precooked for them. Yet on weekends, when Mother is around, the daughter invariably prefers to go off and play with her friends than to be with her mother.

Or take the husband who expects his wife to have the same house-cleaning preoccupations that his mother had. He blames her for being "sloppy." Or the wife who expects her spouse to bring her an occasional flower or a box of candy. Her previous boy friends always did that. Her husband, unaware of this secret expectation, fails to come through and is blamed for being "unappreciative."

Then there is the *"But You Promised"* blame game. This is particularly common in young children or adults who still behave like young children. In this scenario, a usually reliable father or mother promises to do something but for some reason does not do it. The child then displays some hurt, sullen, or pouty behavior, delivers the *"but you promised"* line, and the presumably guilt-ridden parent arranges to follow through. Again one sees an expectation that is not satisfied and blaming behavior added to the disappointment. But don't people have a right to occasionally change their minds? Even on a promise? Haven't you?

In all the above instances, the blamer, disappointed that his expectations are not met, feels resentful and chooses to blame someone else rather than blame (or better yet, acknowledge and reevaluate) his or her expectations. This leads me to suggest a second practical rule for mental health:

Expect nothing and you will have no one and nothing to blame.

If you work at following a rule like this, you will be pleased and gratified when nice things happen and not sour and blameful when they don't. And people are more likely to gratify you because you will be a more pleasant person to be around.

To try to live by this rule means that you have to learn to depend on yourself instead of others. An infant has to depend almost entirely on his environment (parents) to support him. Maturation means slowly substituting self-support for environmental support. Or, in the immortal words of Fritz Perls, the father of Gestalt Therapy, "you have to learn to wipe your own ass."

Many people don't want to do that. They prefer to have others do their work for them. And they try to manipulate them through the blame game known as *"Why Are You So Selfish?"*

A wife doesn't like driving in congested traffic and is reluctant to learn to deal with these conditions. She asks her husband to drive her to a department store on a Saturday. He would rather watch a football game on television. She responds with a *"Why are you so selfish?"*

A man wants to see a movie. He is self-conscious about going alone. Rather than struggling to overcome this, he asks a friend, whom he has accommodated many times in the past, to accompany him. The friend would rather not. His reply? "After all I did for you, *why are you so selfish?*"

Don't be tricked if you are the intended victim of this *"Selfish"* game. And if you practice it, see if you can give it up. Because what the accuser is really saying is: "Please *my* self instead of *your* self." You, in short, are being accused of being selfish in the hope that your guilt will make you satisfy the other person's selfishness.

Remember. There is nothing immoral about being self-seeking. You *are* a self and you have a right to seek your self's satisfactions, pamper your self, actualize your self. If you don't, who else is going to do it for you? To be self-*ish* (involved in satisfying *your* self) is perfectly reasonable and respectable as long as it is coupled with *honesty*. To say "I want," "I need," "I desire" to another person is quite aboveboard, providing you grant the other guy the right to say "Yes" or "No." It is only when self-seeking goes on in a disguised way, where your dealings with other people have a *hidden* agenda, that it becomes a manipulation. Like when you do a man a favor with the unspoken assumption that he will pay you back. And when he doesn't, you accuse him of being "selfish."

Blame is used at other times as a way of avoiding self-examination. One young man I know counters all criticisms by blaming the person who is criticizing him. If he should be accused of being dishonest in a particular situation, he will counter with "Well, you're dishonest too." If he is accused of unfairness, it is "You were unfair yesterday." If someone tells him he resents something he just did, he responds with "There are a number of things I resent about you, too."

At other times we resent and blame others for displaying qualities that we are not willing to accept in ourselves. Some years ago, while engaged in reform Democratic politics, I was feeling especially resentful toward another politician, of similar political persuasions, who was making my work irrelevant. I, as a psychiatrist, had first gotten into politics as a matter of principle, and I resented this "opportunist" for being so "personally ambitious" and pushing aside a coalition that I headed. What I failed to appreciate at the time of my blaming game was that I had evolved my own political ambitions and that I was also taking advantage of "opportunities" to further them. And that this man, whom I blamed, was simply more successful at it than I was.

A married couple have a fight. It begins because the wife feels irritated with her husband over something. They go to bed that evening without saying a word to one another. She is no longer angry and would like her husband to contact her, talk to her, reach out to her, caress her. He, not knowing that her mood has passed and fearing that she is still resentful, does nothing of the sort—preparing to wait it out until she gives some indication of reacting to him more kindly. She is not willing to reach out and make contact herself, although she would like to. Lying there, she begins to blame him for not "making-nice"—for not doing something she is unwilling to do.

Tom was a very poor manager of money. He failed to pay many of his debts. One day, while he was out, an agent from a department store came and repossessed a television set. When Tom returned home, his immediate response was to blame his wife, Betty, for letting the agent in the house. This was easier for him to do than accepting responsibility for his own shortcomings. When Betty grew angry at these charges and told him that his failure to pay the bills drove her to distraction, he continued to slough off personal responsibility by escalating the blame to a new level.

"If it was that important to you," he said, "why didn't you lock me out of the house until I paid the bills?"

In-laws are good ones for playing another version of this same blaming game. Take Tom again. His mother, Charlotte, blamed daughter-in-law Betty for Tom's financial straits, although Betty was actually a very thrifty person. Charlotte preferred to blame Betty's nonexistent "extravagance" rather than to confront her son or accept her own responsibility for raising him to be financially unreliable.

Blaming reactions, like others, tend to run in families. Like Tom, one picks up the pattern from one parent and repeats it. But please, please, don't blame it on your parents if you are a blamer. They learned it from their parents. Besides which, the purpose of the blamer in all of the above examples is to affirm the idea that "I'm not responsible, *you are.*"

If you are a blamer, a good rule of thumb is to presume that *everything that happens to you is your own doing.* Whether this rule is absolutely true is irrelevant. The fact of the matter is that you will progress far more rapidly along the road of self-discovery and ultimate contentment if you think along these lines than you will if your attitude is one of "I'm not responsible, *you are*." For in any living situation, the only person you have any real control over is yourself. If something goes wrong in your life, it is less likely to recur *if you can see the part you played in it and avoid repeating that role in the future*. If someone else is "responsible" for your fate, only he can alter it. But once you begin to accept responsibility for your life (including your disappointments and mistakes), *you* are in a position to change it.

Some of you may read this and say, "But I *always* accept responsibility for everything that happens to me." That, too, is your doing. You needn't *always* do that. You could just as readily see how another person plays some part in what happens to you. If you live with a blamer and accept all the responsibility, you don't deserve any medals. You could just as readily rid yourself of the blamer.

I suspect that those martyrish types who always dutifully accept blame use the same strategy that Smiley, our family Airedale, employs. Whenever anyone yells at the cowardly creature for any real or imaginary misbehavior, she lowers her head, peers up at him contritely, puts her tail between her legs, lies down, rolls over on her back, and displays her belly. It is as if she were throwing herself upon our mercy. "I did it. I'm wrong. Look how ready I am to admit it and accept my punishment." In this way she disarms even her harshest critics.

Blame can also be used to avoid closeness. Many couples play a perpetual blaming game. They don't get along. They would, according to the wife, except that her husband expects too much of her, criticizes her housework, never shows appreciation. It would work out, says the husband, except that his wife is too critical of the time he spends in the office, nags him about the house, doesn't bother keeping the house tidy, and objects to his friends.

When couples relate in such a way, at least one of them is using the blaming game in order to justify staying at a distance physically. They no longer bear their partner any love, yet are afraid to say so, afraid to leave and live life on their own. They aren't sure they will do any better. Yet they don't want to be intimate with their unloved spouse. So they continue to live with him or her, all the while expressing dissatisfactions and then using these dissatisfactions to justify their physical distance.

If you find yourself living with a perpetual blamer, you ought to do some serious soul-searching as to why you remain coupled to such a person.

As absurd as blame is, whether of self or others, I offer the following exercises—some of which involve playing the blaming game. I do this only to help you get free of blaming behavior. I am guided in these selections by some of the experiences people have had in Encounter Groups and Gestalt Therapy groups, and by the writings of such psychiatrists as Ronald Laing. Briefly stated, the idea, paradoxically, is that you best overcome a troublesome condition by fully identifying with it and living it out.

EXERCISES

1. Write down a list of five major and five minor disappointments (both present and past). Next, stand in front of a full-length mirror, grimace at yourself, wag your finger, and blame yourself and curse yourself for all these disappointments (i.e., "It's all your fault . . . only you . . ." etc.).

2. Next, using this same list, stand in front of an empty chair. Imagine different people in that chair and blame them for the same disappointing experiences in the same manner. Accuse them aloud. Exaggerate if you wish.

3. See whether you are more comfortable blaming others or yourself in the above exercises. Work with more instances of disappointment in the area of blame you are *least* comfortable with. See if you can make a game of it—and if you can become aware in general of the game-playing aspects of blame.

4. Become the people you blame. Try to identify with their sense of innocence, their sense of being victimized. See if you can emotionally get into defending "yourself" (the person you are playing) aloud.

5. Finally, repeat the listings of disappointments that you've made aloud, and add "No one is to blame" after each one. Grant everyone else the *right* to disappoint you. Grant yourself (in the mirror) the right to disappoint yourself and others.

6. Copy the following Gestalt Prayer. Place it on the bathroom mirror. Read it each morning and evening at tooth-brushing time:

> I do my thing, and you do your thing.
> I am not in this world to live up to your expectations.
> You are not in this world to live up to mine.
> I am I, and you are you.
> And if by chance we find each other, it's beautiful.
> If not, it can't be helped.

7. Carry a notebook about for one week. Jot down every negative reaction you have toward yourself ("If only I had . . . why didn't I . . . how come I did . . . what a fool I am for . . ." etc.) and others ("What a rat he is for . . . how dare she . . . doesn't she *understand* that . . ." etc.). Write these things down in your book as soon as you can. Immediately ask yourself what *expectation* you or the other person isn't fulfilling. See if you can't then give yourself (or him) the right to be as you are

(or he is). Reread the list nightly. See if you can't do for yourself what you expect others to do for you.

8. Make a list of the people you blame most for your lot in life. Rank them in order. Wherever possible, make an appointment to see them and tell them that you don't blame them any more. If you can't see them, phone or write. If they have passed away, imagine them in an empty chair and forgive them aloud.

4

THE STRATEGY OF NO STRATEGY

WE are all looking for some satisfaction out of life. Some of us think that it will come with success.

"Once I am successful, all my troubles will be over."

To one person success means money. To another it means fame. To a third it means power. To a fourth it means having an ideal lover.

To achieve success, the strategy-seeker adopts a game plan. If he is in business he will wheel and deal continually in an attempt to make the big buck. If she is an actress she will spend hours making agents rounds, auditioning for shows that have little merit, visiting the "in places," and entertaining the right people so as to ingratiate herself with agents, producers, and more successful theater people. If the success-seeker is a politician he will pass countless hours in meaningless debates, shake thousands of anonymous hands, and devote a great deal of time and energy in planning to thwart, defend himself, and retaliate against his political rivals. The seeker of a perfect lover will run through date after date after date, devoting much time and attention to getting people to fall in love with him or her.

There is an ancient Buddhist saying: The only thing worse

than not getting what you want is obtaining your heart's desire. And these success-seekers seem to prove this adage nearly every time out.

For what happens when the anticipated success is finally realized? After a short initial period of satisfaction, life goes on for them in the same worrisome way. The businessman anticipates and strives toward even "bigger" successes. The actress, after achieving stardom, starts to worry about her *next* role. The politician who achieves power is always looking over his shoulder, worrying about those who would like to take over his job. And the love-seeker, after he or she has attained perfect love, begins to find flaws in the relationship and starts working toward obtaining an even "finer" love from somebody else.

The reasons for this? All of these people have gotten so caught up in working for tomorrow's success that when tomorrow finally arrives they are unused to accepting it. Their modus operandi has become one of "working toward a fuller future." They've gotten so involved in the activities, rituals, and strategies of their striving for success—they've become so *conditioned* to performing these tasks—that they are left with an empty feeling if they can no longer perform them. They can't enjoy their success when it arrives because their "future" orientation has made them lose contact with the *here* and *now*. The *means toward achieving the goal* have replaced the *goal* as a life style.

I have a close friend, a bachelor in his early thirties, who is a businessman. He is perpetually worried about his business, concerned about expansion, miffed at competitors' practices. He works incredibly long hours and complains of having little free time to "unwind, relax, and enjoy myself." A few weeks ago he told me dejectedly of missing out on a deal that would have brought him in "really big money."

When I questioned him about his business, he conceded that if he sold it, he could realize a profit of three hundred thousand dollars—enough to live on for the rest of his life. Yet he would no more sell his business than he would give it away. His business life, as dissatisfying as it is, is the only way of life he is used to. And he is still searching for "some really big money."

As uninspiring as these "success" stories are, consider how even more unfortunate are people who plan and plot and strategize for a "success" that never comes. Those who work at jobs they don't like, hoping to get a promotion that never comes. Those who ingratiate themselves with people they dislike, hoping for a favor that never arrives. Those who perpetually put off what they feel like doing today for a tomorrow that never dawns. Those people who do achieve "success" at least have an opportunity to realize the bankruptcy of their ambitions. Most of them are so caught up in the merry-go-round of success strategies that they are unable to stop going in circles. But a few, with considerable courage, manage to throw their "success" away and try to look for something else in life in order to achieve a sense of fulfillment. And that fulfillment, when they find it, comes from living fully in the *here and now*.

Just what does living in the *here and now* mean? It means living fully in the moment and for the moment, and becoming aware of everything going on inside of you and in the world about you. It means making today as rich and rewarding as you can. It means doing what you feel like doing instead of what you are "supposed" to do. It also means giving up plans, gimmicks, ploys, and manipulations designed to assure some questionable future success.

Does this mean you have to quit your job in order to find contentment? No. Not if you can find some satisfaction in it.

Or if it is necessary at the moment in order that you may provide yourself with other *very clearly defined* current-day satisfactions. But if your work isn't rewarding you certainly should not get overinvolved in it. You would be far better off working less often or looking for another job that is more satisfying.

Does living in the *here and now* mean that you shouldn't plan for the future? Again the answer is No. You can't help but give some thought to the future. Yet it is surprising how often the future seems to take care of itself if you are living fully in the present. For when the "future" does come, it will occur in some future "present" that you will once again be living fully in.

Living in and for the present does not imply that your life won't follow an orderly progression. It will. Nor is it shortsighted. For the existential philosophers have demonstrated there *is* only the present. The "future" is merely a concept that never arrives. The past is a "present" that was, and is recalled *right now*—in this present—and as a response to something going on in this present.

Life is, in many ways, like a song played on a flute. It follows its own pattern, has its own rhythm, yet you never hear more than one tone at a time—a tone that continually changes as the moment changes. When you most fully enjoy listening to music, when you really get "into it," you become totally involved in the present sound, in the immediacy of experiencing it. You don't anticipate the note after the next, but enjoy the richness of the one you are hearing. Similarly, those who get the most out of their lives have also acquired the habit of tuning into and savoring their own present "note."

And just how does one live in the *here and now*? Well, it requires a bit of retraining and reconditioning. It means making contact with *where you are and what you are doing in the present* instead of spending too much time daydreaming. When you ride the bus or take a train, it means becoming aware of those around you instead of burying your nose in a newspaper. It means being aware of what is missing from your life, then and there, instead of fantasizing about lying on the beach at Waikiki. If you are driving home, it means fully appreciating the road, your movements, and the sound of the engine, instead of rehearsing a conversation regarding what you will tell your spouse. And when you see your mate, it means being open to whatever he or she brings up and whatever you wish to say *right now*—unrehearsed and quite spontaneous—instead of some prerecorded message you worked on in the car that might be irrelevant to the present situation.

Above all, living in the *here and now* means being yourself instead of preplanning events. It means *adopting the strategy of No-Strategy*.

Why have no strategy? Simply because it is impossible to plan a "success" strategy in matters of work or love. Trying to make yourself into the sort of person who will be loved by others never brings satisfaction, as John Stevens so aptly put it, because even if you are "successful," you never know if you are loved for *you* or for your *act*. You always are on stage and can never be comfortably yourself.

Moreover, act as much as you will, there is absolutely no assurance that your strategy will work. Suppose you decide to "impress" a woman you are dating so as to win her favor. You take her out for an expensive dinner, treat her to a Broadway show, take her home at night, and simply kiss her at the door so that she won't think you're simply out to bed her. You call her for future dates and find she is perpetually busy. Why? Perhaps she doesn't like being "impressed" with fancy dinners. Maybe she would have preferred to stay home and talk. She might even have felt you to be too unaggressive sexually. Between your date and your phone call, she might have fallen in love with the telephone repairman who, after coming over to fix her phone, didn't leave until he spent an hour making love to her.

So the next time you date someone, your strategy is to try the "aggressive-male" approach. Only you find that this doesn't work either. The new lady is offended by what she considers to be your premature overtures.

The same holds true for women who employ strategies in order to woo a man. You try to show you have common interests. You talk of sports and politics. Except that this man may be looking for someone with different interests than his own. He might find that more stimulating. Or you employ a sex strategy. You plan not to go to bed with him for at least three dates so as to keep his interest up and to show him that you value intimacy highly. Except that he is turned off by your hard-to-getness. The next time you meet a man you like, remembering your earlier experience, you try to show him how much you like him and yield your bodily favors almost immediately. Except that this chap takes you for granted as an "easy lay."

The same failures of strategy occur time and again in work situations. One office worker tries to impress her boss by her diligence, arriving early and leaving late, and her willingness to follow his instructions without argument. But the promotion goes to someone else who simply works a nine-to-five schedule. Why? She gave her opinions whenever she felt the boss's instructions were impractical. However, another boss might regard Miss "Talker-Back" as an upstart and give the promotion to Miss "Quiet Hard-Worker."

These strategies can become very confusing indeed. Some

people, failing at alternate strategies, unwarrantedly assume that there is something wrong with *them* and that's why they are not succeeding. They lack the self-confidence to realize that it is, more often than not, just a question of the breaks of the game—that they have simply failed to connect with someone who appreciates them for what they are. And, if they are always putting on acts, it becomes difficult for other people to know just *who* they are.

When I was an adolescent, I felt myself to be unpopular. I watched and studied other people who seemed to have it made. One boy told lots of jokes, so I told lots of jokes. But I still felt unpopular. Another excelled scholastically. I tried that, but again felt the strategy to be a fiasco. Another did poorly and always got in trouble with the teachers. So I tried that, too, with no better results.

Later, as a psychiatrist, I met lots of these same "popular-student" types as patients of mine. And what a surprise. In their teen-age years they had felt as out of it as I did.

In truth, on reevaluating my adolescence, I found there were some people who liked me. But I wasn't living enough in the *here and now* to appreciate it. I was trying for even greater "success"—to be "in" with those "on top." And I was as indifferent and oblivious to those who admired me as those whom I admired were toward me.

I shall give you another rule for mental health that you shall just have to take on faith:

If you are truly yourself, you will eventually find people who love and respect you.

I believe that there is a buyer for every human characteristic under the sun. Some of us like aggressive people, others passive ones. Some like them fat and some like them thin. Some like intellectuals and others prefer earthy types. Some want talkers, others listeners. People, unfortunately, are able to disguise their characteristics in misguided attempts to market themselves more readily. Can you imagine the fix we would be in if ladies' dresses could do the same thing?

I can imagine a rack of dresses in Macy's. Some are long-skirted, others are minis. Some are of lace, others of cotton. Some have low necklines, others high ones. Some are striped, others are prints. One silk minidress is hanging on the rack, watching different women come in and make their selections. The first three dresses sold have long skirts. "Maybe I'm not good enough," she thinks, and grows her skirt longer. The next few women buy striped dresses. "I think I'll change my print to stripes," she says, and does so. A low neckline is purchased next. Our ever-changing dress changes her high neckline for a low one. Then, cruelest of blows. Another lady comes in and falls in love with a silk print minidress with a high neckline—a sister dress that was hanging next to our heroine on the rack. Our heroine has a nervous-dress breakdown on the spot.

The moral of this story is: *Be seen, but be yourself. Sooner or later someone will want you.*

And one more rule for fully living in the *here and now*:
When you are dissatisfied, ask yourself what it is that you really feel like doing right now. And try to do it.

The following procedures, if performed, should help you live less in fantasy, more fully in the *here and now*, and help you to adopt the strategy of No-Strategy.

EXERCISES

1. For the next week, spend fifteen uninterrupted minutes each day contacting yourself. Focus your attention on everything going on inside of you. Make silent statements to yourself beginning with "Now I am aware of . . ." Notice how you are

sitting or walking. Become aware of your posture. Check out the muscle tension in your face, around your mouth, in your jaws, neck, shoulders, chest, belly, and arms. Become aware of the muscles around your anus and genitals. And in your legs. Breathe into the tense parts. Tense them up still further. Then see if you can allow them to loosen up. Focus attention on your breathing. Is it full or shallow? Regular or irregular? Sense your heartbeat. Become aware of your clothes as they contact your body. And the air as it touches your skin. Finally, become aware of your daydreaming, as it diverts your attention from what is going on inside of you.

Vary these fifteen-minute sessions at different times of the day and in different places. In the morning, afternoon, and evening. In the shower or bath. In bed or out walking, standing, sitting.

2. Spend another fifteen minutes each day for one week contacting the outside world. Close your eyes for part of the time and see how many different sounds you can identify. Open your eyes and silently describe to yourself everything that you see ("Now I am aware of . . ."). Notice the environment (the sky, trees, buildings, streets, litter). Focus in on these objects and see how many new structures you can perceive inside each of them. Become aware of the people about you. Describe to yourself their facial characteristics (color of hair, eyes, skin texture, blood vessels), clothes, their postures, gait, etc. Do you look at their whole bodies or do you permit yourself to view them only from the waist up?

Again, perform this task in different places—alone, with strangers, with friends.

3. Spend one full day becoming aware of your daydreams. When and where they occur.

After each pleasant daydream, ask yourself: "What good thing does the daydream supply that I am not getting out of my current life?"

After each unpleasant daydream, see if you can't discover some unfinished situation in your life where you held back and didn't express yourself fully.

See if you can't correct these situations.

4. Write a composition on what you want from other people (friends, mates, employers, employees, associates, parents, children) and the roundabout ways you have of asking for these things. Write about one person at a time and write quickly at first, without thinking. After the spontaneity is gone, work deliberately at finding your indirect ways of asking for things. If you can come up with nothing, ask the people involved how they feel you indirectly ask for things. Listen without explanations or defenses and thank them when they have finished.

5. Take the above listing of what you want from others, and see if you can ask for these things directly.

   (It may involve something as "minor" as *declaring*, "*I* want to go to a movie," instead of *asking*, "Would *you* like to go to a movie?")

6. Spend an entire day doing exactly what you would like to do. Throughout this day, ask yourself, "What do I feel like doing *now*?" and do it.

   It may involve your wanting to be alone or with people. To see a ballet or a pornographic film. To call a friend or tell off an enemy. To buy yourself something to take a bubble-bath. To sleep late or take a trip.

   What you feel like doing from moment to moment will change, of course, and it is up to you to check in with yourself repeatedly to make sure you are doing what you want to do at that very moment.

5

REJECTION

ONE of the most important lessons for you to master in working on yourself iş learning to reject what (and whom) you don't desire and learning to accept rejection from others. This is an extremely hard task for many people. Yet it is hard only because we attach so much symbolic meaning to the word No.

What you have to do is learn to say and accept "No" as a simple statement of preference—the way a child says "No," if he doesn't like his spinach or doesn't care to play—and learn not to read too many meanings into it. The exercises at the end of this chapter should help you learn to do this.

Many people find it almost impossible to say "No." Take Ted, for example. A friendly, gregarious, charming sort of person with much charisma, he seems always to exude warmth and a sunny smile. He invariably has a host of plans, projects, and ideas that he is working on, and all of them involve his being with other people. He likes to talk with other people, and consequently has a great circle of acquaintances. Whenever anybody asks him to meet with them he routinely says "Yes." The problem is that he becomes so overcommitted that he is constantly breaking his "Yes" commitment. He will phone back repeatedly to change a meeting time because he has just given your time up to another's request.

Or he'll arrive hours later. Or he'll just forget all about your appointment, apologize afterward, and make a new commitment to you that only goes through the same hopper. He has succeeded in establishing a reputation as a "nice guy," of course. But his full reputation among those who get to know him is that of "nice guy who is unreliable and irresponsible."

Eleanor, another charming person, is a psychotherapist. She, too, tries very hard to be helpful. Whenever anybody has a problem, she volunteers to help out. She says she will lend you money, give you a lift to a neighboring community, or will watch your children if you are away for a weekend. She is full of things that she *will* do, because at the moment she is usually busy. "Give me a call tomorrow, just before you want to go, and we'll arrange it."

When you call her tomorrow, however, she is usually not in. You leave your number with her answering service because you either have to hear from her by five P.M. or make other arrangements. She returns your call at five-thirty, after you've changed your plans. "Oh, I'm so sorry," she says. "Those damn answering services are so unreliable. They just now gave me your message."

When I first met Eleanor I was most impressed with her. She seemed to be a skillful fellow professional, warm and quite generous. Of course, I had never asked her for a favor, although I had seen her offer her time and efforts to many others. One day, quite incidentally, I mentioned that my wife and I had to be out of town one weekend and that we were looking for someone who might watch Smiley, our dog.

"I'd love to do it," she said. "I'll even be in your neighborhood that Friday evening giving a lecture. Why don't you phone me that afternoon and I'll arrange to pick Smiley up. I just love dogs. Have two of my own and I'm sure they'll get along just fine."

I called that Friday, but couldn't get through to her. I spoke to her sister, who was driving her to the lecture. She promised to deliver my message. Several hours passed without a call back. I left word at the place she was speaking. My luck was no better.

Fortunately we were able to make other last-minute arrangements for Smiley. But when I saw Eleanor the following Monday I was irritated.

"Why did you do that?" I asked. "You didn't have to offer to take Smiley if you didn't want to. And why didn't you phone me back so I could make other plans earlier?"

She offered some lame excuses for not returning the calls that were illogical and quite unexplainable. But she was still so *committed to her image* of being *a generous lady who was true to her word* that she turned on me, quite angrily, denied that she had ever promised to take the dog in the first place, accused me of calling her a liar, and stalked out of the room.

End of our relationship.

Eleanor, so far as I can gather, is still losing potential friends in the same way. Those who stick by her have learned not to take her "generosity" seriously.

Alice lives in a large apartment house and has two young children. She too can't say "No" to people. Neighbors call her continuously, asking if they can drop their children off to play with hers while they go shopping, visiting, traveling.

"Certainly," is her constant reply.

The result? She is everybody's babysitter. Her neighbors think of her as an exceptionally nice woman who loves children. She is perpetually surrounded by scores of playing/ fighting/eating/crying children, and is nearing the breaking point. She may have her reputation, but she shall shortly have her nervous breakdown as well.

Or take the other side of the coin: people who can't take

"No's." I am thinking, particularly, of all those people who never venture out, who never try new jobs, who never initiate contacts with other people (and if they do, wind up being slaves to them), simply because they would be overwhelmed by "rejection."

There are certain occupations where rejection is par for the course. The theatrical professions are a good example. Whether you are an actor, director, playwright, stage manager, or producer, people you approach for work (or funds) say "No" much more often than they say "Yes." People in the theater who realize this roll with the punches, take it in stride, and are not unduly affected emotionally. Many others take it more personally. Perhaps that is the reason many theater people tend to drink more than they should, fantasize more than they ought to, brag, exaggerate and make up stories of their successes, and cattily put others down who have made it when they have not. Not that this pattern is especially restricted to certain theater people. It is prevalent among all those who have not learned to accept "No's" with graciousness and without their egos being out on the line.

Why is it so hard to give or accept a rejection? It's all a matter of conditioning. Historically, most of us were trained by our parents, teachers, and culture to be "nice," and to avoid hurting other people's feelings. We were all duly impressed with the importance of being "liked" by others. And finally, since all of us to some degree or other have been raised to feel Not-OK, getting people to like us becomes a strategy to get OK feedback from other people.

Still, if you don't like something or someone, it is hard to avoid rejecting behavior, no matter how much you try to control it. In fact, the irritation caused by this disguised rejection is often greater than that which would be caused by a simple "No," or a statement such as "I don't like it."

The case of Eleanor, who offered to watch our dog when she really didn't mean to, is a case in point. As are, actually, all the other illustrations of people who irritate themselves or others by not being able to be rejecting in its simplest, most direct terms.

In the spring of 1972, at the age of thirty-seven, I published my autobiography, *A Psychiatrist's Head.* It was a very frank account of my professional and personal life and contained both some tragic and explicitly sexual material. Judy, my wife, had me send a copy to her mother, Betty.

Now Betty is a very decent woman, but also very sexually prim and proper. Two months after receiving the book, she had still failed to acknowledge its receipt. Why? She was offended by the sexual passages, and rather than tell me so (and risk "rejecting" any part of me and thereby "offending" me) she chose to remain silent and thereby reject and ignore the entire *me* as portrayed in my book.

Aside from the historical reasons for "No's" being difficult to give or get, there are the more important present-day reactions that prevent one from taking a more objective view of the situation. These boil down, invariably, not to the rejection itself, but to *the way we interpret it.* As Epictetus put it, in the first century A.D.: "Men are disturbed not by things, but by the views which they take of them."

Albert Ellis, the noted New York psychologist and father of Rational-Emotive Psychotherapy, has based his school's therapeutic approach primarily upon Epictetus' insight. It is an approach well worth understanding by anyone desiring to free him or herself from emotional suffering.

Ellis postulates the "A-B-C Theory of Emotional Disturbance." *A* is the *Activating Event.*

A boy friend, for example, informs you that he is seeing another woman and wishes to end the relationship with you.

B is the *Belief* about the activating event—your interpretation of this event.

For instance, when your boy friend tells you he wishes to stop seeing you, you tell yourself:

"I'll never find another man like him."

"I must really be a worthless person."

"This is *terrible*. Everything always happens to me."

"Since he doesn't want me, nobody possibly could."

"I can't stand the world for being so unfair and lousy."

"That bastard. He shouldn't be that way."

These beliefs (*B*) then cause *C*, the upsetting emotional *Consequences*. In this example, given the aforementioned beliefs, the lady in question feels either *depression* and/or *hostility*.

Ellis' system of therapy involves step *D*, *Disputing* the irrational ideas (*B*) which caused the upsetting consequences. It means telling yourself things like, "Where's the evidence that because this man wants to end our relationship, I'm a worthless person? Or that I'll never be able to have a decent relationship with someone else? Or that I might not even be happy alone?" Or, "Why shouldn't the world be full of injustices and imperfections?"

Using step *D* fully, disputing your "Ain't It Awful" or "Ain't I Awful" immediate interpretation of events, produces *E*, a new *Emotional* reaction. In *E*, you now have a reasonably well-adjusted response of *sadness* ("We had a nice relationship and I'm sorry it's ended, but it did have its problems and now I can go and seek a better one") or *annoyance* ("It's irritating that he's seeing someone else but it isn't *awful* or *intolerable*. It's just one of the imperfections one sees in an imperfect world") in place of the depression or hostility.

This simple but effective process of reasoning with yourself

(*D*) when you have upsetting emotional reactions (*C*) should be engaged in regularly by anyone seriously working in self-therapy. People who are in private therapy (therapy with *others*) usually rely on the therapist to perform step *D* for them. When they can do it on their own, they no longer need therapy. But there is no reason that you can't perform this step yourself and save the expenses of psychoanalysis or formal psychotherapy.

There are two other things to bear in mind if you are the sort of person who suffers rejection poorly:

1. If someone says "No" to you, he isn't necessarily rejecting *all* of you. He may object to certain qualities you have but accept others, and,

2. So what if certain people reject you? As I pointed out in the previous chapter, you can't win them all. Be yourself at all times and someone else is likely to want you.

Before moving on to the Rejection Exercises, I should like to share another personal story with you. While in medical school, I was seeing a psychoanalyst. I was seeing her, most likely, for the same reasons you are reading this book: I lacked self-confidence, felt emotionally turbulent rather than calm, and tried to hide these things by putting on acts. Naturally, feeling Not-OK, I was extremely self-conscious and feared rejection.

I would repeatedly go into my analyst's office and tell her about lost opportunities regarding strange women I had failed to meet. I would pass someone in the street, while shopping, upon the seat alongside me in a bus, in a theater. I felt paralyzed. I just could not approach any of these young women. I was so worried about being turned down, I couldn't even think of what to say. I felt I needed a smooth "line." It never occurred to me to state the plain truth, to simply say, "Hello. You're very attractive and I would like to know you better."

After repeating a version of this story for the hundredth time (and, need I add, analyzing it to death), two things occurred to me. One, that I was very "image" conscious. It was not *I* who would suffer from a turndown, but *how it would look to others*. How it would look to the girl who might reject me. How it would blow the "cool, successful" image I was trying to project. And the second thing I realized was that the real *I* suffered from my *not* making these approaches. Even if only one person in a hundred said "Yes," I'd be ahead of where I was by letting a hundred pass by in silence.

And so, I began to approach people. It took considerable discipline and courage that first time, but then it became progressively easier—as all tasks do when repeated. All this in spite of the fact that my first few attempts resulted in "No's." For what I discovered after the "No" was that I no longer carried the unfinished situation around with me (the "Why didn't I speak to her?" feeling). It was done. Over. If it didn't succeed, it was through no fault of my own. I felt braver and more pleased with myself simply for asking. And, naturally, there were many later successes to come.

Is this something only men can do? Not at all. One woman I know began a very pleasant relationship one day while in a cafeteria. She went in for a cup of coffee, saw an attractive man sitting alone at a table, walked over to him, and said, "You're a very interesting-looking man. Do you mind if I join you?"

This leads me to propose a further rule for mental health:
It is better to ask for what you want and get a "No," than never to ask and insure no gratification.

EXERCISES

1. Write a short composition on the very worst things that can happen to you if you are rejected. Follow that with a short treatise on the worst things that can happen to others if you reject them.

2. Recall some of your important past rejections. See if you can't discuss, again in writing, why these rejections really weren't so awful after all. Even if they are quite recent, and still feel painful, see if you can't get in touch with some positive elements in them—what you learned, what you later gained.

3. Spend one day, saying "No" to all requests that others make of you (unless they invite you to do something that you *especially* want to do). Give no explanations or rationalizations for your "No" other than "I don't feel like it"—and give this answer only if specifically asked why you said "No."

4. Prepare a list of areas in which you are most sensitive to potential rejection. Then see if you can enter these areas and risk your rejections.

5. Ask three people who you are *certain* will reject you to do something with you (have lunch, come to your house for a party, have coffee or a drink, go to a movie, shopping, etc.).

6. Following exercise 5, ask three people whose rejection you are uncertain about to share some time and activity with you.

7. Next, ask three people, you are sure will accept you to do the same thing.

8. Tally your results and experiences in exercises 5, 6, and 7, and write a short composition on what you got out of these experiences.

9. Risk a rejection at work. If you are an employee, ask your boss for a raise and/or some extra time off. If you are an employer, ask an unintimidated employee for a special favor.

6

TOUCHING

THERE is a hunger for *body contact* within all of us that, if unfulfilled, has serious emotional consequences.

Most of the beasts we see show evidence of this same hunger. Cats will slither about your leg until you stroke them. Dogs will jump and lick and roll over on their backs in order to be petted. Horses will approach either one another or men and nuzzle. Monkeys and chimps, the species most closely related to us, groom and touch one another as part of their everyday rituals.

It is modern man, living in our computerized, automated society, who frequently loses the ability to satisfy this basic need. It is seemingly "programmed" out of him. It is no accident that the phrases used to describe many disturbed people are "out of contact" or "out of touch." For you discover, more often than not, that these same people have received (and given) painfully little stroking, touching, and hugging from (or to) others. And this is not necessarily because it is not offered. Quite frequently the remote "out-of-touch" person refuses to accept it.

It seems that the more our society "advances," the more technology and specialization flourish, the more the barriers to body contact multiply.

One need only examine a few "advances" made in my own

field—medicine and its subspeciality, psychiatry—to see the unfortunate side effects of progress made on other fronts.

Take Pasteur's "Germ Theory"—the discovery that many illnesses are transmitted through microorganisms, invisible to the naked eye, and potentially present on any part of a person's body. While this has led to advances in the detection, control, and cure of many diseases, it has also led countless parents to subtly condition their children (just as they were conditioned) to stay at arm's length from their fellows. How many times in the course of growing up have you heard phrases like "Don't drink from her glass, you might catch cold . . . Don't get too close to him, he may have something contagious . . . Wash up after handling money. It's very dirty because so many other people have handled it . . . ?"

Our mouthwash commercials tell us of germs in our mouth. Our soap commercials tell us of germs on our skin. And the new feminine "hygiene" sprays talk of helping keep sexual areas "clean and inviting." It is no wonder that there is very little trust in the natural order of things.

My six-year-old son, Richard, has a great aversion to embracing and kissing (a phase, I hope, that he will grow through). Why?

"It causes germs," he says.

When I attempt to tell him that it is not so, he tells me, correctly, that he saw it on television or heard it from his teacher.

A second example would be Freud's psychoanalytic theories. Apart from the understanding of man that they have given us, they have also contributed to the anti-touching paranoia. For what two men would readily embrace—what two grown women could endlessly stroke and tickle one another (which they did as more innocent and *untutored* children)—when we have been taught that, to use the psychoanalyst's term, the human animal is laden with "latent homosexuality"?

Healing has traditionally been done "by the laying on of hands." Yet I've seen doctors so fearful because of germ theories that they don rubber gloves before *examining* anyone. And as for laying on of hands for a *cure* . . . ? Better to write a prescription for some useless placebo or give someone a "shot."

Medicine, however, contributes only one small part to the anti-touching conditioning. Technological advancements—labor-saving devices—contribute their share, too. We as a society seem to prefer things made by machine to those made "by hand." It is as though hands were going out of style.

You can wash clothes and dishes by machine, set type by machine, sweep by machine, make shoes and cars by machine, sew by machine, prepare foods packaged by machine, reproduce art by machine, and even buy machines to rock your baby. For years people have used another "machine"—a bottle —to feed him.

Other cultures have not lost this ability to touch. Some of these societies we call "primitive," or "tribal." People eat and drink out of common bowls, their medicine men do a great deal of sponging, touching, anointing, and rubbing, and adults embrace and hold one another much more freely than we do. They also wear less clothing, seem to feel less ashamed of their bodies, and offer one another more skin to make contact with.

Other societies—I think particularly of the Greeks and Italians—are much more physical and more *in touch* with one another than we are. It is natural to see two Greek men hug, embrace, and even dance together. It is quite normal to see two Italian women strolling along holding hands. It is par for the course to see parents embracing children and children kissing parents—even when these children have already grown into adults. It is, of course, quite possible that this warmth and spontaneity will ebb as these countries approach the technological "sophistication" of the United States and other parts of Western Europe. But let us hope not.

Several years ago I abandoned a largely psychoanalytic practice and became involved in the new wave of Encounter Group therapy being promoted and taught at Esalen, in California. Shortly afterward, I helped organize (and still work at) Anthos, another such center based in New York City. And what has impressed me most about many of the people who attend groups at such centers is their search for a sense of intimacy to counteract the cultural alienation we live in and have become personally adjusted to. Yet these same people have become so programmed to their own "places" in the system that they need a "leader" to give them permission to touch, hug, and explore one another.

Despite rumors to the contrary, these groups are not hotbeds of sexual activity (indeed, many sexually promiscuous people who never attend groups seem to use sex as the only way they know to satisfy their need to touch). Yet it is easy to see how the public might be misled in view of the media's focus on touching, hugging, and occasional nudeness. For it is true that such "touching exercises" are great initial favorites among many participants who have, for so long, not permitted themselves to satisfy their hunger for body contact.

That body contact is an important *source of pleasure* should come as no surprise to anyone. For pleasure is basically perceived through the five senses. We spare nothing when it comes to *taste*. Indeed, Americans consume more food per capita than any other people on earth. Nor do we deny our sense of *smell.* More money is spent on cosmetics (toiletries, perfumes, etc.) yearly than the federal government spends for education. When it comes to *hearing*, we titillate ourselves with the latest stereophonic, high-fidelity equipment and pay our musicians well to please us. And *visually*, we continuously attempt to surround ourselves with things that please the eye.

Our fifth sense organ—our skin—represents a huge surface area through which to receive pleasure. Anyone who has lain upon a beach can attest to the warmth and good feelings that follow the *sun touching* our skin. Let another person try it, though, and some people will go into an absolute panic.

Too many of us have gotten overly programmed into the "meaning" of bodily contact. For such people, touching is permissible only in matters of love (sex) or war (fighting). You can make bodily contact with such people only if you hit them or have intercourse with them, because *they* don't realize that any middle ground exists. They feel they have to "respond" to a touch in terms of passionate hate or passionate desire. They don't realize that they can simply accept (or give) a touch or embrace for what it is and all that it is.

There are many touch-starved women who will refuse a hug because they are not "prepared to go to bed with the man." And men, too, who spurn warmth from their fellow man because they erroneously assume the other fellow to be a "faggot." Or wonder, if they warmly approach or respond to someone, if they themselves are "faggots" or will be considered to be "perverts" by those whom they wish to express physical warmth to.

Many of our aversions to satisfying our own skins' desire to be rubbed is frequently this concern with "image"—how it will look to somebody else if such contact is allowed. If that is your concern, I can only say again that your goal, in self-

therapy, is to act counterphobically. To work for *yourself* and
not others, you must risk blowing your "image." In the process
you are likely to discover your truest self.

Before proceeding to the exercises, I would like to say something about body shame. While this is not directly related to
problems people have in *touching*, it is directly related to our
attitudes toward our very own skins—the wrappings that we
are packaged in.

In Chapter 2 ("Secrets"), I talked of how anything *hidden*
is likely to foster shame. The same observations hold about
people's bodies. Encounter Group experiences have taught me
that those people who are most reluctant to participate in a
nude session—who prefer to "hide" their skins inside their
clothes—are also the ones who are most ashamed of their
bodies. Some of them will tell you that right out.

"I'm embarrassed . . . I'm too fat . . . I'm too thin . . . My
breasts are too large . . . My breasts are too small . . . I have
an ugly scar . . . My penis is too small . . . I'm afraid I might
have an erection."

Others give different "reasons" for refusing to disrobe.

"I don't see why it's necessary . . . It's not my cup of tea
. . . I only do that in front of my husband . . . I wouldn't even
do that in front of my husband . . . I can't see what I'd get
out of it, anyway."

Still, people in both categories do occasionally overcome
their inhibitions and shed their clothing. And the results are
uniformly gratifying. They begin to feel less self-conscious,
less ashamed, and more accepting of their bodies through
the simple procedure *of not hiding them any more*. In addition to that, feedback from other people usually corrects
many misconceptions and misperceptions that they had about
themselves.

I recall one instance of a young woman who was very ashamed of her "big behind," and left feeling much better after it had been particularly admired and praised by many group members *before* she told of her embarrassment.* Or of an elderly woman who had taken to covering up after having had a breast removed surgically. Earlier in her life she was most casual about nudity and used to swim and sunbathe in the nude along with similarly unashamed friends. When she finally undressed, it turned out that there was almost no evidence of deformity, as her remaining breast was small and sufficient tissue remained after the other was removed so as to make little apparent difference. Here again, the feedback of others lessened self-consciousness and shame.

And finally, there is the preoccupation among men that "my penis is too small." (To small for what? I am always tempted to ask.) I would say that a good seventy percent of men share this erroneous assumption regarding their "status symbol," and it is only through a *shameless* exposure of their bodies that such cockeyed ideas can be corrected.

Many people look better, as a matter of fact, with their clothes off than they do with them on. And I would encourage all readers of this book to work at being more casual about their bodies by being more casual about nudity.

Oh yes. Another rule for mental health:

Touch people more often.

EXERCISES

1. Each day, for the following week, make some sort of physical contact with everyone you talk with. Use handshakes, embraces,

* See *Marathon 16* by Martin Shepard, M.D., and Marjorie Lee (New York, Pocket Books, 1971).

simple touching, while you talk with them, or a casual arm around the shoulder.

2. Ask to have someone tickle (lightly stroke) your back for at least fifteen minutes. Return the favor to that person or extend it to someone else.

3. When you meet a friend or relative whom you haven't seen in a while—and whenever you go visiting people—start kissing them hello and goodbye. Don't discriminate on the basis of sex. If the person you are about to kiss and embrace withdraws, appreciate it as a sign of his "uptightness," not as something wrong with you.

4. Become the *last* one to pull away when you hug.

5. Become aware of the different way you hug men and women. See if you can use the same degree of gentleness regardless of sex.

6. Go to a masseur or masseuse.

7. Give a friend a massage.

8. The next opportunity you have for sexual intimacy, spend it, instead, in touching, stroking, embracing, mutual bathing, and massaging.

9. Sleep without nightclothes for the next week. Allow yourself to walk freely about your home without "covering up" at bedtime or upon arising, regardless of whether your children, parents, spouse, or friends come upon you.

7

SEX

MEN and women everywhere—in ancient civilizations and contemporary ones—have been, are, and shall continue to be preoccupied with their sexuality. Both the phallus and the womb have been worshiped in representations of deities. Every ancient culture has produced its own "How-To-Do-It" Sex Manual (the best known of which is the Indian *Kama-Sutra*). Many of our museums and libraries have special sections—closed to the general public but open to scholars doing "bona-fide" research—containing collected treasures, both from antiquity and the recent past, that depict and document sexual practices. A tour through the Museum of Pornographic Art in Lima, Peru—one of the few such places open to the general public—reveals exquisitely graceful pre-Columbian ceramics (statues, pitchers, and bowls) depicting sexual involvement in any and every form known to modern man. Inca men and women are shown while masturbating, mutually licking one another's genitals, engaging in every recorded position of man/woman intercourse, being sodomized, having homosexual relations, performing fellatio and cunnilingus, soul-kissing, and grouping in threesomes on upward.

So if you happen to worry about being one of those sexually concerned and preoccupied people, the first thing to do is appreciate the fact that you have a lot of company. You fit into the mainstream of human history.

It seems only natural that people would have an interest in exploring, watching, and understanding this incredible thing. This "thing" that can produce—through the rubbing together of two small bodily parts—a rush of sensation that can make you leave your ego temporarily, enable you to fuse and become indistinguishable, momentarily, from another human being. This "thing" that is responsible for *re*-creation.

It is my contention that much of what passes for "voyeurism," "pornographic interest," and "perversion" (all of which, incidentally, are *put-down terms* and are better not used) is simply attempts to grasp the ungraspables—the mystery of how we were born and how we transcend ourselves. And this curiosity is as natural as breathing.

Aside from this nonproblematical interest and investment in matters sexual, there is also the "problem" of people who consider themselves to have sexual *problems*. Here again, countless millions are spent yearly on marriage manuals, sex-improvement books and literature, and psychiatric fees, counseling fees, and sex therapy (*à la* Masters and Johnson) fees.

Those having sexual problems fall, more or less routinely, into one or more of the following three categories. They have either (1) functional disabilities or (2) questions about the appropriateness of their sexual urges, or are (3) looking for greater satisfactions in their love making.

What I should like to do in the following pages is to save you the trouble, time, and expense of buying and reading any of the thousands of books and pamphlets dealing with sexual "problems." I shall present you with the general themes and approaches used in dealing with difficulties in any of these three areas, offer some ideas of my own, and finally suggest some exercises to help you overcome these dilemmas.

1.

Let us start with the *functional disabilities*. In men, this refers primarily to premature ejaculations and impotence (lack of erection). In women, it invariably means frigidity (lack of orgasm).

The first approach to any of these problems is an educational one. Ignorance, fear, shame, and anxiety feed upon themselves, and the first goal of almost every sexual therapy approach is to put things into perspective.

Fact: According to Robin Saxon, the noted British sexologist, most men reach orgasm within two minutes of starting coitus. The *normal* range is ten seconds to three minutes.

If you properly grasp the significance of this statement, it almost proves that *there is no such thing as premature ejaculation*.

Many patients of mine have complained about their premature ejaculation. But when I ask them how long they last, they invariably fall within Saxon's normal range. I have even heard men complain of "coming too quickly" when they routinely last for five minutes or more.

Moreover, this normal range of ten seconds to three minutes is a figure covering *all* age groups. It is another *fact* that younger men reach orgasm faster than older ones. Therefore their normal coitus time is even faster.

When you ask a man complaining of *premature ejaculation*, "Premature for what?" it usually turns out that it is premature for his "image" of what his lasting potential should be. Those who profess that they "come too quickly to satisfy my wife" either know not of what they speak, are trying to satisfy women who have sexual difficulties of their own, or are simply unfamiliar with and/or unaccustomed to bringing the woman to orgasm *prior* to penetration—by means of touching, licking, and stroking. Why? Their "egos" demand that it be done the *hard* way.

As for impotence in a man, it is another *fact* that nearly *all* men, myself included, at one time or another have failed to achieve and/or lost their erections prior to or at the moment of intimacy. There are many reasons for this, but the event itself is so common that it should also be considered "normal." How, then, does it become a problem? It becomes one when a man, experiencing his first episode of "normal" impotency, decides that there is something especially "wrong" with him. In every subsequent encounter with a female he brings "The Big Doubt" into bed with him: Will it happen again?

The result is very much akin to *examination anxiety*: the more you have, the poorer you do. "The Big Doubt" thus frequently acts as a self-fulfilling prophecy.

When I was twenty-four, I began my own personal psychoanalysis. At the time, sex was not one of my problems. I had functioned successfully with a number of women and overcame the usual "quick orgasm" dilemma by making love— on the occasions when I was intimate with a woman—at least twice a night (one "quickie" for me and a longer, second ride for my lady). Sex became a problem shortly after analysis began, however, when I experienced my first failure to erect.

I was embarrassed/perplexed/mortified/apologetic. I believe I even "came" without erecting. The woman I was with was, fortunately for me, both reassuring and patient. We attempted intercourse later that night and to my great relief succeeded. But I spent a good number of hours on my analyst's couch trying to "understand" what had happened. To the best of my knowledge I had a fear of becoming overly involved with this lady. It seemed as though successful coitus would symbolize a "marriage contract" of sorts and I didn't know if I was ready for that.

This woman and I did proceed to live together for two years. Since the problem of dysfunction never returned, sex again ceased to be a "problem." But when we separated, every time I shared a bed with a new woman, every time I hoped to impress her with my ability as a lover, I again brought in "The Big Doubt"—along with the anticlimactic apologies/excuses/explanations in those instances where I failed.

Back to the analyst's couch once more. Since I functioned well with some women and poorly, initially, with others, I had my analytic work cut out for me. And I came up with a second "reason" for failure: many of the women I was "intimate" with I really didn't *want* to be intimate with. I was proceeding, too often, out of habit. Or I might find a woman attractive and appealing with her clothes *on*, but when they came *off* there was either some physical quality or aspect of her embrace that turned me off. Yet what do you say to a naked lady? I couldn't say "No," but my penis could and did. On still other occasions I might fail over *guilt*—feeling that I was "cheating" on someone else.

Yet for all of my understanding of the *reasons* for failure, the "problem" wasn't solved until the day I woke up and realized that my penis has a mind of its own and that I no longer had to offer excuses for it. If I was with someone and it "didn't happen," well, it just didn't happen. No further conversation was needed. The event spoke for itself. And what happened next was most interesting. When I no longer cared that much, the occasional dysfunction disappeared almost entirely.

And I discovered that not only does my penis have a mind of its own, but that *I do too*. That true sexual freedom means not only the right to have intercourse *with whom* and *when* you choose, but it also allows you *not* to have intercourse *whenever you choose not to*. One of my proudest sexual memories is of a time when I was in bed with a new woman whom I felt attracted to *before* we got into bed but unaroused by *afterward*. And instead of going through my usual routine of trying to turn myself on to this ready, willing, and able woman, I simply said "I really don't feel like making love," got dressed shortly afterward, and left.

The big functional difficulty for women is, as most everyone knows, lack of orgasm. So again we must start with a *fact*:

Most women, most of the time, fail to achieve orgasm when they are intimate.

And what happens to some women to make the *normal* lack of orgasm a problem? The same thing that happens to men. They bring their "problem" into bed with them, undergo the same *examination anxiety* ("Will I pass the test *this* time?"), and suffer the same self-fulfilling prophecy.

What are the "cures" the experts offer for these functional problems? They vary, somewhat, with the "expert" you are reading or talking to.

The so-called premature ejaculator is encouraged to raise the threshold of excitement either by deadening the sensation in his penis (by wearing a condom or by using a topical anesthetic salve—such as Nupercainal) or by diverting his attention from the sexual act itself. In this second approach he is advised to concentrate on his breathing, or think of a baseball game while being intimate. Or he is told to try various mechanical approaches, which vary from lying quite still inside the woman after initial penetration or when he feels his orgasm approaching, to nearly pulling out *or* pulling out when he becomes hyperexcited, to having the woman squeeze his penis firmly *behind* its head until his excitement is quieted.

Any and all of these approaches work for some people. My own inclination, however, is to suggest that *if* you insist on working on the usually illusory "premature ejaculation problem," you stick to the mechanical approach. This won't get you into any trouble (possible allergic reaction to salves) and may, actually, increase your technical repertoire. But I can't see why anybody would want to divert his attention from the exciting qualities of sex by thinking of something as prosaic as Tom Seaver's earned run average or the last World Series game between the Orioles and the Pirates.

In the past the "cures" offered for frigidity and impotency ranged from reassurance to advice to get "help" from a psychoanalyst, psychotherapist, or marriage counselor. What usually happened was that the sufferer went in to see an "expert," presented the sexual problem, and was then encouraged to talk about his or her parents, spouse, children, and other interesting, but often highly irrelevant subjects. The results often failed to justify the fees charged.

Dr. William Masters and Mrs. Virginia Johnson achieved a great breakthrough in making the public realize that anywhere from fifty to eighty percent of these "problems" could be cured within two weeks of direct sexual work. Just what does that work involve? It boils down to *learning to live in the* here *and* now; *learning to appreciate what* is *instead of what* isn't; *living in the moment and letting the future take care of itself.*

Their approach is simple and self-evident, and fits perfectly into the general approach of this book. What they do is interrupt the cycle of *failure, fear about future performance,* and *guaranteed future failure*. They start off by banning attempts at sexual intercourse for about a week. During that period of time their patients are instructed to "pleasure" one another. What this means is that they are instructed to touch and be touched, rub and be rubbed, massage and be massaged, stroke and be stroked. It is against the *rules* for it to *lead anywhere*. This forces people to *stop anticipating* how it will all come out, and *start appreciating* how warm, rich, pleasing, and stimulating simple body contact can be. And when you really get into allowing your *total body* to turn on, the genitals, more often than not, take care of themselves.

In every significant way, the Masters and Johnson approach is no different from that of Bernard Gunther, Esalen's master of sensory awareness, or Cindy Shanks, his counterpart at Anthos. These people teach other people how to touch and appreciate touching. Gunther's book, *Sense Relaxation*, could profitably be read and employed by anyone suffering from frigidity or impotence, for he presents dozens of sensory-awareness exercises. The essentials of what he has to teach have already been presented to you in the previous chapter.

In addition, women who don't experience orgasm ought certainly to attempt masturbating to orgasm. If they simply try it long enough and in different ways, ninety percent of them will get there. When they do manage to find the way to "push their own buttons," there is no reason at all why they can't share this information with their lovers.

2.

Our second category of sufferers are those concerned with the *appropriateness* of their sexual urges. They either have *desires* or *aversions* that they consider to be abnormal.

They may dwell on the possibility of being intimate with somebody other than their spouse. They might think occasionally of having a homosexual liaison. They have urges to experiment with oral sex, anal sex, multiple sex (involving three or more people), or sexual positions other than the Momma/Poppa arrangement (male on top, face to face). And they are torn between these desires and various degrees of guilt, ignorance, or fear.

Here again the initial approach of most experts in handling such problems is an educational one, followed by counseling that changes as cultural norms change. One starts by pointing out the facts.

Fact: Over ninety percent of American husbands and sixty percent of their wives are likely, in the course of their marriage, to have an extramarital liaison.

Fact: Over eighty percent of men and women have had at least one homosexual *experience* (intimate body contact with someone of the same sex) by the time they reach maturity.

Fact: There is nothing hazardous about anal sex provided personal hygiene is observed before and after intercourse.

And when it comes to oral sexual practices, the same holds true. Semen is biologically sterile. It is composed mainly of proteins and fructose, a five-carbon sugar—substances that any dietician would gladly recommend.

The vaginal secretions are also primarily composed of proteins. They do not naturally give off any unpleasant odor. On those rare occasions of a heavy odor, it is invariably a result of either failing to wash away the secretions from the sweat glands in the skin of the groin, or from some nonspecific infection that is not, in any event, spread by oral contact.

Fact: Group sex has, according to all current authoritative literature,* transcended the hippie/idle-rich/greatly impoverished classes and become part of the middle-class, middle-American way of life to increasingly large segments of our society—both on a private and individual basis and through "swinger" organizations that publish their own periodicals, run their own clubs, operate their own bars, and sponsor their own parties.

Fact: Whatever things the sex experts, counselors, analysts, and therapists may *disagree* on, all would agree that *restricting* copulation to the Momma/Poppa position is quaint (as are bustles, petticoats, and the campaign buttons of Calvin Coolidge) but entirely unnecessary. Any and all positions that please are "permissible."

What can these sufferers glean from the above facts? They can realize that if they should choose to side with their desires (as opposed to their inhibitions) and act on their impulses, they will be acting in numerically good company. They won't be giving in to something "abnormal" if they choose to have an extramarital affairs or to experience a homosexual contact, for it is, statistically speaking, the "normal" thing to do.

One of the great inhibiting fears of the extramarital affair is that it might place one's marriage in jeopardy. But this is never the clear-cut issue it seems at first glance. While it is true that an affair *might* cause a separation, so might self-imposed fidelity. For such a program often makes the self-disciplined mate resentful toward the spouse in whose name he or she stifles other sexual impulses. Besides which, unfinished business—strong impulses that aren't fulfilled—have a nasty habit

* See *Group Sex* by Gilbert D. Bartell, Ph.D. (New York: Peter H. Wyden, Inc., 1971).

of preoccupying your attention to the point of driving you crazy.

Also, when you feel strongly impelled to have an extra-marital affair, you often can't tell whether the strength of your desire is related to the desirability of your potential lover, *or* to some ill-defined but unsatisfying aspect of your marital relationship that *makes your urge so strong*. Having the affair often enables you to find out. Intense passions have a way of passing, rapidly, when satisfied. A deep love will endure many trials.

To have or not to have a homosexual experience also deserves some discussion. When my wife, Judy, read the draft of this chapter she found it hard to believe the percentages of people who have had homosexual experiences.

"That never happened to me," she said.

"What of that story you told me about the time you dis-covered masturbation?" I asked. "How another girl came over, told you and your friends about it, and tickled and touched you all."

"That wasn't homosexual," she answered. "We were only nine years old. That was just fooling around. It was a new discovery. We were just exploring something new."

Yet that is all that a homosexual experience is, really. Our fear of having such an experience comes from the emotional connotation of "degeneracy" that the term *homosexual* has for many people. It is as if one touch, one lick, one caress, with our mirror images would brand us for life as "untouch-ables." Or that the experience would become addictive.

"I might like it too much," I have heard people say.

But of course, that is absurd. If you do something and like it, you don't feel badly for having done same. Because in that feared "future" you are enjoying yourself.

Also, given the "heterosexual" nature of childhood conditioning and the prevalent social attitudes in much of the Western World, one is unlikely to "choose" a homosexual rather than a heterosexual life style after sampling both. Otherwise a majority of our population would be *practicing* homosexuals. And of course they are not.

But I recognize and appreciate these unfounded fears. I had them myself. It was not until I was thirty-five that I allowed myself my first homosexual experience.* For me, as for Judy, it was "a new discovery. We were exploring something new." And it has not particularly interested me since.

It took me thirty-five years of living to be unconcerned enough about my image to allow myself this new contact. I see that my former aversion to this and its absence from my experience were based mostly on fear and self-doubt, and not on my "manliness" quotient.

As for desires (or aversions) concerning licking and sucking one's partner, and/or swallowing, sniffing, or spreading his bodily secretions on you, I can see nothing in the practice that goes against man, God, or nature. Observation of other mammals will convince a skeptic that they, free, unfettered and uncultured, fully exercise their instincts to smell and taste one another. Only man, with his cultural hangups, seems to have problems in this area. But with some intelligence and the capacity to act counterphobically, there is no reason that you can't overcome these limitations.

There is a richness and immense satisfaction that can come from fully immersing yourself in your partner. When one is in love, love's fluids anoint. Lovers who fully accept their *own* bodies are glad to share any part and its by-products. Lovers willing to accept such parts of their partners, reaffirm the dignity and goodness of the body.

It disturbs me when I hear of people having aversions to love

* See *A Psychiatrist's Head* by Martin Shepard, M.D.

making during a woman's menstrual period. There's nothing unclean about it. Nor is there anything amiss in attempting cunnilingus at such times. Yet the same people who would be "shocked" and "offended" at the suggestion of getting menstrual blood on their tongues would think nothing of ordering steak tartare or a rare roast beef, thereby gorging themselves on the blood of some bull or cow that has been dead for several weeks.

All cultures tend to encourage conformity. People who question the "appropriateness" of their sexual urges have, perhaps, extended this conformity to their nonsexual lives as well. While all of those people who question the appropriateness of their sexual desires must make their own decisions regarding whether to go with their impulses or their cautions, I would point out that Ronald Laing, along with many other contemporary psychiatric theorists, postulates that the best way to overcome your preoccupations is to live them out.

I, for one, agree with Laing. Such ideas were stated, most succinctly, years ago by Oscar Wilde:

The best way to resist temptation is to yield to it.

3.

What, finally, is the approach toward those looking for greater satisfactions—for a bigger bang—out of their sex lives: those who are bored, tired, or have found themselves settling into some mechanical routine?

The experts suggest a standard prescription, which makes eminent sense. *Schedule time* for sex play as you would for more "serious" pursuits, such as work, reading the newspapers, cleaning the car. *Break out of your routines* surrounding intercourse. And *expand the number of roles* you play.

Varying *routines* is not too difficult to do. If you always make love at night, try it in the mornings or at lunch breaks. If you follow some set ritual of kiss/touch/pet/copulate, vary it. If you always draw it out—hasten it (and vice versa). If you undress yourselves, undress one another. Or keep your clothing on. Positions and practices can be altered, as can locales.

You can make love in cars, on deserted beaches, in motel rooms, in the woods, in bathrooms, in showers, on the floor, in the dining room, and sitting on a chair. I am sure that you need no further help in expanding this list.

By "expand the number of *roles* you play," I am referring to changing more basic patterns and attitudes. It means that men and women have to learn to make contact with the other sex inside themselves—for the man to contact the "woman" in him, and the woman the "man" inside. It means learning to enjoy passivity if you are a man. And allowing "aggressiveness" to emerge if you are a woman. This requires more concentration and work than simply varying your *routines*, but also brings greater rewards. For you then have a chance to incorporate and enjoy the sexual satisfactions open to all people and not just the stereotypical ones "assigned" to men or to women.

The man who can approach orgasm by having a woman play with his breasts knows what I am talking about. As does the woman who can boldly initiate the sexual contact and guide, glide, grab, and thrust herself upon her receptive mate.

For all of the printed material concerning sex—from erotic literature to books and articles dealing with "sexual problems" or "finding fulfillment"—some words are in order concerning the problems that the sex literature itself creates.

For starters, there is the myth of the "sanctity" of the simultaneous orgasm. While most authorities are content to lay this erotic fairy tale to rest, myths die hard. For most of the marriage and sex manuals published up until the late 1950's sang hymns of praise to the glories of "coming together."

Not that there is anything *wrong* with coming together. That's fine. But so is coming separately. The problem of the simultaneous-orgasm approach is that lovers have to take mental stopwatches into bed with them—adjusting their movements, caresses, pauses, and lunges—so as to attain "ultimate bliss." Naturally enough, they often fall short of their goal. The result of that is *disappointment*.

This disappointment and dissatisfaction is the other side effect of our "helpful" sexual literature. It tends to make people focus on *what they have not*, instead of helping them to enjoy what they have. You can read about some new form of sexual bliss and become dissatisfied with your own activities because you conclude you're not "there" yet.

The worst fallout results from the thousands of articles written about the female orgasm. The "How To Achieve Five Orgasms a Night" or "How To Achieve a Stronger Orgasm" type article. Any woman who takes such articles too seriously is in danger of *losing contact with where she is and what she feels* while in the sexual act because she is *anticipating* an experience. Sex can be quite rewarding for a man or a woman if he or she is fully savoring the *here* and *now* experience of it. Indeed, the climax can even be anticlimactic, because it ends the period of aroused excitement. But if a woman starts to worry about frequency or the strength of her yet-to-come orgasm, she leaves the pleasure of what she *has* and gets into the anticipation of what *hasn't yet arrived* or the frustration *of what isn't happening*.

I would like to close this discussion with another mental health rule:

People are responsible for their own orgasms.

This rule means that while making love, you make love for yourself, first. You ask for what you want and you tell your partner how to please you if he or she is not already doing so. And if your partner is not satisfying you, it is up to you to find some satisfaction or to find another partner.

I know that much has been written about the importance of being considerate of your partner while making love. Yet the best lovers are the ones who transmit *their* enjoyment and excitement to their partners. For they are primarily pleasing *themselves*, and in the process, usually please their partners, too.

While considerateness is always a desirable quality, I would insist that even this trait comes about through the paradox of sexually considering yourself first. For it is only after you have truly learned to satisfy yourself that you can stand back dispassionately enough to be sexually helpful to another human being.

People, unwittingly aided and abetted by the sexual literature, start to get into the "My Orgasm Is Better Than Your Orgasm" game. Climaxing and performance become a status symbol, in the same way that cars, clothes, and houses can be. And if you don't compare your climax with someone *else's*, you tend to compare it with others that you have had. Sure it's easy to have great sex on a weekend away from home. It's different when the kids are around or the phone may ring. But if you can get into the moment *as* the moment and *for* the moment—and when that moment passes get into the next moment, without comparisons—you are home free. Some times you may have sensational petting and a fair orgasm. Other times this is reversed. Still other times you have neither. It is *something else*. That's not so bad. That's what *is*.

I think a new definition of the female orgasm would be helpful:

An orgasm is the best reaction you are capable of in any particular act of love making.

If you are a woman and can work on remembering that definition, I believe sex will become an even more rewarding experience for you. For it stops the comparison game and helps you get in touch with the pleasures of what *is* happening.

EXERCISES

1. Write a short composition on "Why I won't let myself be sexually freer." In addition to stating your reasons, also write of how your life would change *if* you were totally free. Elaborate (don't end abruptly with "then my boyfriend and I would split up," for example, but go on to fantasize what would happen *after* that).

   When you are finished, reread your story and add a short one-sentence moral to it.

2. What are the things you would never tell your partner about yourself, sexually, and why?

   Take a risk and tell.

3. For the next three nights, schedule an early hour or two in bed with your partner. There is to be no intercourse on these nights. Instead, on the first night, you are to become aware of what sensations pass through you when you allow intimate body contact *without* using your hands. You may lie against each other in any variety of ways, breathe against one another, rub backs, bellies, or toes, lie quietly, or move.

   On the second night, contact can only be made orally— by licking, nuzzling, kissing.

   On the third night, touch might be used as well. But avoid

mutual masturbation. Instead, stroke, massage, caress, embrace, and tickle. Get as much into the moment as you can.

4. Think of all the things you normally wouldn't ask of your sexual partner, and ask for them.

5. Play an opposite role in bed for the next week. If you are passive, initiate things and be active. If you are usually active, try being passive in all aspects of your mating.

6. Spend one day "reversing" your sex, attitudinally. When you awaken that morning, lie in bed and imagine your body undergoing a sex change. Dress in your usual way and perform your usual routines, but do them in word and deed the way you would expect someone of the opposite sex to do them. If you are a man and conceive of a woman as being gentle, or catty, or seductive, or touchy, or sentimental, or subservient, *you be that way* around both men and women. If you are a woman and see men as being outspoken, aggressive, crude, tough, braggarts, initiators, or planners of activities, *you be that way.*

   Play your role throughout that day and night, including the time you spend in bed at night with your mate. Again be true to form (for instance, you as a man might lie on your back and be mounted by your woman, who would also play with your breasts).

7. Spend two nights in which you do everything you can to please your mate sexually on night one, and in turn have the same services performed for you on night two. On night one, you are a total giver. On night two, a total receiver.

8. Follow up exercise 7 by employing alternate orgasms on the same night. The man should pet, lick, and caress the woman to orgasm, and then let her do the same for him.

9. Think of your favorite unfulfilled sexual fantasy. Then, by asking for it, try to bring it to realization.

10. List all of your sexual aversions and the things you have never tried. See if you might not try them at least once.

8

AGGRESSION

SEX and aggression are reputed to be the two big bugaboos that every human being has to learn to come to terms with. I have dealt with the question of sex at some length in the preceding chapter. I do not intend such a long discussion on aggression.

Why? Because I think that the problem of aggression is actually overrated. When I say "overrated," I am not referring to problems of nations at war or the hoodlum who might assault you on your way home tomorrow night. What I am referring to is your learning to deal with your *own* aggression. For if you learn to say "No" when you don't want something, take "No" with grace from others (see Chapter 5), ask for what you want, and say what you feel, there isn't much leftover tension for *aggression* to pose any great problem.

The phrase "Make love, not war" implies much the same thing. People who are being satisfied, who are tuning in to and enjoying the pleasures of life, don't operate under the frustrations, resentments, and tensions that lead others to assaultively aggressive and warlike behavior. Any reader who has conscientiously followed through on the work outlined in the first seven chapters of this book can, I am certain, attest to the fact that he or she feels less irritable and on edge now than before starting self-therapy.

"That's all well and good," I can fantasize your saying, "but I still find myself quite irritated at certain times and I would like to discharge that feeling as quickly as possible. So what do I do about that?"

"It depends on the circumstances," I would answer.

Some people seem to hope for a day when they shall never have any angry and aggressive feelings. That is not only unrealistic but *unnatural.* All human beings are capable of angry responses. If you doubt it, try hitting your finger with a hammer. The "Oh, *shit!*" reaction is just as strong and real as the pain that accompanies it. Or recall the last time you felt put down, insulted, or physically abused by someone else.

The hallmark of a *naturally* angry response is that once felt and *expressed*, it passes. If it smolders/lingers/bothers you beyond a short period of time, chances are you are either caught in a frustrating living or working situation, and/or are ashamed of expressing your hostility, and/or project your own disliked attitudes onto other people and hate *them* for it.

Life situations that fail to offer satisfactions lead to perpetual disputation and anger regardless of how well you can express these feelings. It is essential, then, to resolve disputes among people you deal with every day—be they parents, spouse, or fellow workers. The paths to such resolution are (1) saying what *you want* in the relationship and expressing *what you feel about the relationship now*, (2) *listening* to the other party's wants and feelings, and (3) *either agreeing* to meet one another's needs *or seeking someone else* whose attitudes are more compatible with your own.

The bind is that most chronic disputers are unwilling to compromise *and* unwilling to call it quits and find somebody else whom they might enjoy more. They thereby put themselves in the bind of continuing to demand from the other person what that other person is unwilling to provide. The result is continuous frustration, placation, quarreling, tears, foiled manipulations, and the inevitable, ever-present, *resent-fulness*.

How do you handle this type of anger? You fish or cut bait, as the saying goes. Compromise or separate. There really is no acceptable alternative. While forcing such a decision by having an honest confrontation with someone else is risky, it seems preferable to the timeless blind alley you otherwise find yourself stuck in.

Other people have a problem "handling aggression" for the very reason that they attempt to "handle" it instead of expressing it. They typically have a great investment in playing the role of "The Nice Guy." They continuously sit on their minor resentments, which therefore build up greater power, which, in turn, requires Mr. or Ms. "Nice Guy" to work even harder at keeping the lid on.

Historically, such people have been made to feel like "Bad Guys" for having angry emotions. Dore Previn, the composer and singer, tells a story of a friend of hers who was so ashamed of his angry feelings (and, therefore, so overburdened by them) that he would rent a small plane and, when airborne, discharge his pent-up feelings by screaming and shouting his head off—up in the sky where no one could hear him.

The "cure" for this type of anger? Let it out. This means conscientiously working at expressing the supposedly "petty" and "irrational" resentments you have.

There have been a number of therapeutic techniques developed to help people get in touch with the forces of anger within them. They involve simple procedures, such as screaming, shouting at the top of your lungs such words as "No" or "Fuck you," pounding pillows, or lying in bed and throwing a temper tantrum.

These exercises by themselves won't solve your problem.

What they will do is help you discharge excessive resentfulness and make it easier for you to express it with people whenever and wherever it comes up. This is where the conscientious work comes in. Let me give you an example.

A dentist friend of mine, Bill, a "Nice Guy," was working at attempting to come to terms with his anger. One day a patient called who had a severe toothache. Bill was planning to go away that day and suggested a colleague that his patient might see. The patient, however, implored Bill to see her, as he was one of the few dentists she had any confidence in. Being a "Nice Guy," he changed his plans and gave her an appointment two hours later.

Two and one-half hours elapsed before she called back apologetically. Her husband couldn't get the car started to drive her to her appointment so she had gone to the drugstore, gotten something for the pain, and obtained temporary relief. She could wait until Bill's regular schedule resumed next week to see him.

My friend accepted her apologies with an "I understand," hung up the phone, but shortly afterward his annoyance got the better of him.

"She could have called earlier," he said. "Or taken a taxi."

Five minutes later he called back his patient and expressed his resentment.

"It was a great step forward for me," Bill said. "In the past I used to sit on things for weeks and feel miserable. Now I've discovered I can let it out after five minutes. Soon, I can even see myself getting mad *on time*."

What Bill did was work conscientiously on his problem. Such work means that if you have *unfinished* resentful business with anyone, you go back to where you left off and follow through at finishing it. If you do that, you will eventually come to the point where you live in the *here* and *now* and get angry *on time*. You will get little things off your chest as they arise and won't let them build up to the point where you have "explosions."

The final "problem" of aggression concerns projecting onto others your own hidden qualities and then disliking them for these qualities. The sort of thing I talked about in Chapter 3, when I resented a politician for his "opportunism" and "ambition" partly because I was unwilling to accept my own opportunism and ambition.

One sees this same process operating in young toughs unwilling to recognize their softer natures who intensely dislike (and occasionally assault) "longhairs," "peaceniks," and "faggots." Or in virtuous prudes—unwilling to accept their sexuality—who dislike those "promiscuous young tramps." Or even shy, self-conscious people, who won't own up to their capacity for arrogance and exhibitionism and so secretly hate others who more readily exhibit these traits.

The "cure" for this problem of anger is to learn to identify with the quality you hate in those people you are angry with.

Not paying attention to this type of anger means that you have parts of yourself *outside* of yourself. You are, to that extent, a less complete person. And so, my mental health rule for this chapter is:

Whenever you feel in conflict with someone, play out both sides and become the person you are angry at.

By that I mean you should try to identify with the person you resent. You become him for a moment when you attempt to think as he thinks and feel as he feels. This is one of the principal techniques of Gestalt Therapy, for the very reasons just elaborated upon, and is most helpfully and readily applied in Do-It-Yourself Therapy.

EXERCISES

1. For the following week, set aside a half-hour in the late afternoon or early evening and run through the following series of exercises:

   a) Tighten all the muscles in your face, extend your tongue as far out of your mouth as possible, raise your hands and make two fists, take a deep breath, stretch, and tense your mouth muscles as tightly as possible and shout/shake/and continue to tense your muscles as you let your breath slowly out. (If you fear that the noise might frighten your neighbors, close the windows and turn the radio up full blast to muffle the sounds you make.)

   b) Shout emotionally charged angry words such as "Shit!" and "Fuck you!" Try to get into feeling the fury behind the phrases. Continue for a full two minutes.

   c) Lie on your back in bed, kick your feet up and down alternately while simultaneously pounding your hands (with clenched fists), shaking your head from side to side, and yelling "No!" over and over again. Do this for several minutes until exhaustion sets in.

   d) Set a pillow in front of you and pound it with your fists while yelling "You bastard!" repeatedly. If someone comes to mind that you resent, pretend that he is the pillow. Continue to pound at "him" as you shout out all your grievances and resentments.

2. For the next few days, become aware of the times you feel *someone else is angry at you.* (It might help if, at the end of the day, you reviewed each day's activities.)

   Whenever you think you experience someone else's resentment toward you, reverse things and ask yourself, "What might *I* be angry at *him* for?"

3. Make a list of all of the people in your life you have resented and hated. Put them in an empty chair in front of you and tell them all off, aloud and in detail, one after the other.

4. After *completing* exercises 1 through 3, try spending a week catching yourself whenever you feel annoyed with someone and, like my dentist friend, expressing your irritations. If you didn't do it at the time, do it as soon afterward as you can. Work toward getting angry *on time*.

5. Following completion of exercise 4, work at playing both parts of all conflict situations you find yourself in. A good way to do this is by placing two chairs across from one another. When you sit in one chair, you are yourself and you address the empty chair as if the person you couldn't stand were in it. Say whatever you feel, holding nothing back. Then switch and become that person. Argue back at the first chair, which you now pretend that "you" are in. Keep a dialogue going, switching chairs as soon as you temporarily run out of words for each character you play.

6. With pencil and paper, list all of the traits you dislike in people you live with or are otherwise close to.

   Write down specific instances of ways in which you display these same characteristics.

9

PARENTS

LEARNING to accept your parents as people in their own right—different and distinct from you—is a task that poses difficulties for quite a large number of people. There should be nothing surprising in all of this. For we all have one very good historical reason—our childhoods.

The infant is born into a world in which he is, literally, *part* of his mother. Without her to comfort, clothe, feed, and shelter him, he could not survive. During childhood our little girl and boy still depend greatly on their parents. They have not yet acquired the skills necessary to provide for and sustain themselves. This is a time one learns certain "do's" and "don'ts." You learn how to count and how to read, how to cook and how to sew, how to hammer and how to saw. And you learn *not* to swallow iodine, *not* to put a fork in the electrical outlet, and *not* to cross a street unless you look to make sure there is no traffic approaching.

Typically the child's contract with the parent is one in which he accepts the dependent role in return for the favors/protection/guidance/and support he receives from them. There are, of course, dissatisfactions. He prefers taking things out to play with more than he does putting them away. He wants to do and try things he sees grown-ups doing and resents it when they say "No." He may want to come and go more freely than they are ready to allow. And he'd rather watch television than do his homework or practice the piano.

Adolescence marks the years during which relatively accepting and "sweet" children become adults in their own right. Following the sexual maturation of puberty, adolescents typically reject the dependent contracts that as children they had with their parents. It is a period of much storm and strife, both in the inner life of the adolescents and in their relationships to their parents. Opposition/confrontation/argumentation are a natural part of the process as the adolescent seeks to break away and find his or her own adulthood. If it is accomplished smoothly, and the adolescent truly feels adult, he comes to accept his parents as he would other adults. If they share common interests and *if* the parents accept him as an adult (not only as their child), they may remain close. If their interests are not similar and/or if the parents cannot transcend their *roles* as parents, there is a polite distance—as any adult would have with people who are on different wavelengths. This second alternative is a more common outcome of maturation.

What I have described thus far is "normal" maturation. Many individuals, no matter how old they are, never make it, psychologically speaking, past either childhood or adolescence when it comes to relating to their parents. Those stuck in the childhood phase remain overly docile and dependent. Those stuck in adolescence relate to their parents in a perpetually rebellious and ill-tempered way.

Given the cultural roles males and females are assigned (males presumably being "aggressive" and females "passive"), one might expect that women are more likely to become stuck in the childhood state and men in the adolescent one. And—although there are many reversals to this expectation—such is usually the case.

Louise is a good example of such a child/woman. In her childhood and adolescence, her parents were perpetually available to her. They were quick to comfort and pamper her. They always soothed her hurts, took her side, indulged her fancies. She, in turn, pampered their egos by letting them know how exceptional they were, how they were the only people who understood her, how much wisdom and sage advice they had, and how appreciative she was.

At twenty-two she married for the first time. Her husband, Greg, was an insurance salesman and just out of college. He was a decent, responsible, upright young man, who looked forward to supporting Louise and raising a family. But it never worked out that way.

Louise was incapable of accommodating herself to the rigors of a more spartan and independent existence. She consulted her mother daily, both to ask for advice on simple housekeeping chores and for consolation over any minor inconveniences she was having with Greg. She was incapable of sticking to a budget and so, behind Greg's back, ran to her physician father for extra funds to pay her charge-account bills and indulge her passion for clothes, cars (which she insisted on changing yearly), and innumerable redecoration schemes.

When her first and only child was born, her parents hired a maid for her. And Mother came over daily for several months to help out and give advice.

After three years of marriage, Louise left Greg. Marriage didn't conform to her picture of "picket fences and lace curtains." She was interested in playing more and working less. Her parents were sympathetic. They agreed with Louise that Greg was "cheap," "selfish," and that he "always got his way." Besides which, Mother was willing to raise Louise's daughter while Louise went back to school and tried to find a new man.

Now thirty-nine years old and on her fifth husband, Louise

lives in another city. But she still phones her family a few times each week.

Sam, who is twenty-eight, is the sort of person who typifies adolescent "stuckness." For he remains continuously close to, yet antagonistic toward, his parents.

While attending a local college, he, like many other students, began smoking marijuana. Not content to do it privately, he naturally let his parents know of his activities. They were frightened, shocked, and strongly disapproving. Sam, rather than dropping the subject, continued to let them know of his usage by smoking at home. Quarrels/insults/door-slamming occurred frequently on both sides.

Dinner conversations to this day are reminiscent of the popular television series *All in the Family*—with Sam typically attacking his father's political and social points of view and Mother acting as a harassed peacemaker.

Four years ago Sam moved out of his parents' home but continued to bring home his laundry for his mother to wash. His attitude was sullen. If his mother inquired about his life he would give her flippant answers or accuse her of trying to hold on to him. Yet he made it a point to inform his parents of many of his activities that he knew they objected to—his dating a woman of another religion, his intention of quitting a promising job, his experimentation with LSD.

Every now and then he would ask his father for a loan or the use of the family car. He felt it was coming to him. On those occasions when his father refused him, he always had some unkind words for the old man.

Two years ago he married. He made it a point to tell his mother not to interfere when she offered to help care for Suzy, Sam's daughter, who was born eight months ago. But whenever Sam and his wife, Brenda, have a party to attend, Sam calls up his mother, expecting her to be always available for babysitting. When she is not, he accuses her of being a hypocrite for having offered to help out earlier.

How can you tell if you are *stuck*, in any respect, regarding your parents? One way is to see if they embarrass you. Perhaps you don't want your parents to meet your friends because you fear they will act in a way that will humiliate you; that they will treat you as their little girl or boy, correct you, or behave "coarsely" in front of your friends.

Such embarrassment is often related to your still feeling yourself a *part* of—an extension of—your parents. You fail to realize that if your parents do react absurdly, it is *they* who will be laughed at, not you. Unless, of course, you take it as personally as a thirteen-year-old who brings her first date over to the house.

Other indications of dependency are the making of routine daily or weekly telephone calls to your parents, wanting their approval constantly, or finding that there is "no other person as good, wise, and kind to me as my mother (or father)."

Signs of rebelliousness are so self-evident, emotionally, to the sufferer, that they need no further elaboration.

There is a certain validity to a child's blaming a parent when things don't work out to his satisfaction. After all, the parent *is* in charge. If a meal doesn't taste good, the child can't very well cook his own. If the family moves and the child must give up his neighborhood friends, that is the parents' responsibility, not his. *But once you pass the age of eighteen*, those conditions no longer hold true. There is no further need to depend upon your parents.

The task of both the *child-stuck* and *adolescent-stuck* person is to get *un-stuck*, by learning to do things on your own and, in doing so, becoming a more self-sufficient human being. You

can't have a very good self-concept—can't very well consider
yourself any person's equal—if you remain a child-at-heart
in relationship to your parents. Whatever *advantages* there are
in taking things from your parents by continuing the "child"
or "adolescent" integrations are more than offset by the loss
of basic self-esteem that results from staying in that role.

The "child" is reluctant to go *through* the adolescent, rebellious, phase. The "adolescent" is reluctant to achieve total
self-sufficiency. He wants all of the advantages of both childhood *and* adulthood, but none of the disadvantages of either.
"Adolescents" are too embarrassed to admit how much they
still *want* their parents, and how much they might even love
them.

Both groups ask for their parents' support and approval
(albeit in different ways) long after they are capable of man-
aging their own lives. Not only does this interfere with their
lives in general (witness Louise and Sam), but it certainly
prevents the possibility of their establishing a realistic present-
day relationship with their parents.

I've talked frequently in this book about living in the *here*
and *now*, and how emotions, people, and relationships change.
One of the things that can certainly be said of people who
have trouble dealing with their parents is that they are usually
reacting to *memories* of both their parents and themselves—
as they all were ten, fifteen, or twenty years ago—and *not*
in terms of the realities of all of them *now*. This is always
due to the *holding back* of the maturational process.

We are left, therefore, with many adults who still *blame*
their parents for the way they have treated them. As if their
parents had *chosen* to make the child's life miserable.

Yet there are very few parents who *intentionally* act cruelly.
Every set of parents, if they could choose, would elect to be
the world's best parents.

Of course, lack of "intent" does not mean that parents don't occasionally act cruelly. Why shouldn't they? They are primarily *people* before they are parents. All of us are capable of cruelty. Besides, they had parents who "misunderstood" them, too. Parents, like all people, can be tightfisted, generous, disappointing, helpful, indifferent, funny, tender, or short-tempered.

When I was twenty-five and a student in medical school, I was still reacting to my parents as an adolescent. I resented having to go visit them each week. I felt that they were still trying to control me. When I was questioned by my analyst whether the situation might not be reversed—whether *I* might not be trying to control *them*—I realized that I made my weekly sojourns to pick up a weekly allotment that they were generous enough to offer me. And that I could possibly manage to get by with a much lower amount. And that I needn't show up weekly to "pay my dues" for their generosity—that they gave it out of kindness and not for my weekly shows of obeisance. With that realization I stopped my mechanical visits, cut down on what I was receiving, and began to relate to them more adultly.

A therapist friend of mine was treating a young man who constantly fought with his mother. He wanted her approval, but she was constantly critical. Mother was an exceptionally irrational woman and never saw how much her son wanted her blessings. He, in turn, could not accept her irrationality.

My friend asked his patient the following question: "If you passed by a mental institution and saw your mother looking through the barred windows on one of the floors, and she was screaming the same things at you, as you passed by, that she now screams at you at home, would it still trouble you?"

"No," said the young man. "I'd discount it, because I'd know she was crazy."

"From now on, then, every time your mother gets on your nerves, I want you to recall that picture of her shouting from that hospital window."

His patient did just that and found his aggravation and frustration subsiding.

A device such as this is, I think, a useful tool for people who find themselves continuously fighting with a non-accepting parent.

Another rule to bear in mind that will help you to see your parents more realistically, is:

Grown-ups are merely children in aging skin.

When you get to feeling overwhelmed by your parents' (or parent substitutes—such as bosses or teachers) "wisdom" or resentful over their "shortcomings," try to see the child that is hiding and acting inside of them. Doubters of this rule need only recall watching General Westmoreland (a little boy playing soldier) or Richard Nixon (another little boy play-acting at being a leader of men) on television in order to understand what I am talking about.

I have purposely avoided writing a chapter on *being a parent* —on dealing more effectively with *your* children—for a number of reasons. One is that there *is* no way to be a *parent*. You can only be *yourself*. And if you become a mentally healthy adult (as, I'm sure, all of the readers of this book are trying to become), you will do all right both as *yourself* and as a parent.

As a psychiatrist, I have seen hundreds upon hundreds of people complaining about their parents. If they were given a great deal of material advantages, they would complain that "my parents bought me things as a substitute for love." If they were given few things, the complaint was "my parents were cheapskates and didn't love me enough." If they were given a great deal of freedom by their parents, they would lament that their "parents weren't interested in me or what I did." But if they were closely supervised, it was because "my parents were too strict."

Naturally it helps to be kind, tolerant, and understanding of your children. Remembering your own childhood helps. But sometimes a spanking or some punishment may well be in order.

So there are no suggestions I have to offer you as a parent, except to bear in mind that *whatever you do, it is likely to be wrong in your child's eyes.* But when and if your child grows to maturity—if he or she doesn't get stuck in childlike or adolescent behavior—your child will come to appreciate that you did the best that you could.

And further—it is your *child's* responsibility to grow up, to mature—not yours to do it for him. Just as you must realize that you are no longer part of your parents—that things aren't *their fault*—your child has to learn the same things about you.

The exercises that follow attempt to help you continue your own maturational process vis-à-vis your parents. You may need *repeated* work on the exercises in order to abandon your unrealistic views of both yourself and your parents. For you must, eventually, learn to let go of them, give up your demands that they be different than they are, forgive them their faults (and all of the things that they "should" have done, did do, and didn't do)—and come to realize that your parents couldn't possibly have been anything other than what they were and what they are.

EXERCISES

1. Again, work with two empty chairs. Put your father in one and tell him all of the negative things you've held back from

him—your resentments, frustrations, hatreds. Be as specific as you can. Then, switch seats, be him, and respond to "you." Say how you feel hearing all of these negative things. Keep the dialogue going by changing chairs once more and telling your father what you needed, now need, wanted, and now want from him. Have him respond by saying what he needs and wants from you (past and present). See whether or not you can achieve any greater understanding of one another's positions, as you keep the dialogue going, as opposed to finding yourselves simply *arguing*.

2. Repeat exercise 1, substituting your mother for your father.

3. Pretend you are your father and write a short composition about "The Difficulties I Had In Raising My Child."

4. Repeat exercise 3, but now write as your mother instead of your father.

5. Place your father back in the empty chair. Tell him all of the things you've appreciated or loved about him. Switch seats and, as your father, say what you *feel* about your child's telling you such nice things. Keep the dialogue going.

6. Repeat exercise 5 with your mother.

7. Be your father and tell your child all the things you've loved and appreciated about her (or him). Switch chairs, be yourself, and say how you feel about hearing these things. Be your father again and respond.

8. Repeat exercise 7 with your mother.

9. List all of the secrets concerning your private life that you would never tell your parents. Place each of your parents in an empty chair in front of you and tell each one, in turn, these secrets. Be your parents and react. Again, keep switching chairs and get a dialogue going. See whether you can move toward mutual understanding rather than conflict and confrontation.

10. If your relationship with either parent is characterized by dependent routines, daily or weekly phone calls or visits (if

you are living away from home), take a month's vacation from these activities. Don't call. Don't visit. Politely tell your parents that you simply want to see what it's like to live without such regular contact with them. And stick to your word.

If you are over twenty-one and still live with your parents, spend the next month living elsewhere, giving the same reasons. Move in with a friend or series of friends, into a Y, a hotel room, with a sibling, or with a different relative. Better still, try all of these different living arrangements for a few nights each so that you might see what it is like to live in different places and different spaces.

11. If your relationship with either parent is characterized by aloofness or grumpiness, or if you have not had much contact with them in some time, see what it is like to try to get closer.

Make a date to meet them somewhere and treat them to a dinner. Give them a small gift—a token of your "appreciation" (whether it is felt or not). Ask them details about their lives. Tell them whatever things you appreciate or like about them—and work hard at avoiding unkind words during this experience.

A day later, write about your experience. Describe what it meant to you and what you learned from it.

If either of your parents is dead, do the above exercise in fantasy for the one (or ones) you can't bring along in reality.

10

ROLES

We are what we pretend to be, so we must be careful about what we pretend to be.
                          from *Mother Night* by Kurt Vonnegut, Jr.

THERE are two perspectives from which to view the *complete* man or woman—the so-called mentally healthy person. We either say that such people are *free* of roles, or that they are capable of playing any and all roles. Either definition is correct and, as far as I am concerned, can be used to describe the same person.

I realize that many people will take issue with my definition. "If someone is playing a *role*, he is not honest—not authentic," they might retort. "I wouldn't want to relate to someone who is putting on an *act* with me."

"Neither would I," I would answer. "But that's not what I'm talking about."

When I define a complete person as someone who *is capable* of playing all roles, I place my emphasis on that person's *ability to enter into any role as a response to any given stimulus*. Thus you can *play the part of* the "Gracious Lady" when you are spending time with someone you like, but can also be the "Angry Bitch" when somebody does you dirty. You can *act* "Helpless" when you don't know how to do something, and like a "Know-It-All" when you do. If you are sexually attracted to a man, you can become "Passionella." But if someone comes on to you whom you don't like, you can show him the "Thanks, But No Thanks" routine.

This ability to *play all parts* is what is otherwise known as "spontaneity." When we say that someone is putting on an "act," we are usually describing someone who *can't* play all roles. Such a person has, instead, a very limited number of roles he can comfortably play. Hence he is typecast and known by his predominant role.

Thus the "Know-It-All" person *cannot* get into the "Helpless" act even when he doesn't know something. Such a person will never admit his ignorance, or the fact that he was wrong about something. Instead he will give justifications for his error.

Why will such a person not acknowledge helplessness? Who knows, exactly? Perhaps because he, as a child, was *expected* to know everything. Or because he was presumed to know nothing, and wanted to prove this was not true. Or because he felt insecure about life in general, and having "answers" for everything—however illusory—gave some sense of comfort and security.

The same circumstances apply to people who have a reputation as "Angry Bitches." They are unable to play the "Gracious Lady" role. Again, the reasons for this may vary. Being *gracious* might be a sign of love, and our "Angry Bitch" might feel that showing love makes her vulnerable. Or she might play the "Angry Bitch" because of having suffered unusual physical cruelties as a child; the residual effects still spill out, uncritically, on all other people.

People who are said to be "inauthentic," "phony," or "acting," are thus acting out "Johnny-One-Note" routines. If they could expand the number of acts in their repertoire, so that the *act* might be more appropriate to the *stage setting they find themselves in at the moment*, they would transcend their role as actor and become "the spontaneous person" (otherwise known as "the complete actor").

Whatever the historical reasons for your sticking to a particular act, the major present-day reason for maintaining it is simply that *you know the part*. Not only that, but *you have never tried playing a different role*. It is the unfamiliarity with new roles that must be overcome if you hope to live a fuller life.

If you persistently play "Helpless," even when you know something, and you decide that it is about time you mastered the "Know-It All" routine in such situations, you wil discover that you feel peculiar/false/unnatural/phony when you first play the new part.

"It isn't me," you might say.

Of course it isn't you—*yet!* But if you play a new role often enough, it starts to feel more and more "like you." And when you truly master it, it becomes as much "you" as your current "natural" *act* is.

The anxieties you feel in attempting new roles are no different than those that an actor of light comedy would feel if asked to play Hamlet for the first time. And yet, the only way to grow as an actor is by trying to stretch your ability to portray different types of characters. I believe that the same principle of growth holds true for people who are not in the theater.

If an actor had to play Falstaff and only Falstaff for his entire professional life, he would soon become quite bored with the part of the clever buffoon. If a citizen continues to play only one role in his life, he doubly suffers. For he is trapped not only by the repetitiveness of his act, but by the *opposite act he is suppressing*.

Thus a person wedded to the role of "The Martyr" can never allow himself to put his own interests first. Similarly a person who insists on playing the part of "The Sane Man" is always haunted by the possibility he may go crazy. For *the only person who can go crazy is one who has a preconception of what sanity is.*

We need, then, to go beyond our stereotyped acts—to abandon our *images* of ourselves—in order to establish to ourselves *who we really are.* If we are afraid of making a fool of ourselves, if we worry about seeming silly, it bespeaks a reluctance to give up our self-image as a rational, competent, stable person. One of the ways, then, to both appreciate and go beyond our present act is to *explore roles we are reluctant to play.* This exploration shall be one of the tasks given in the exercises that conclude this chapter.

Before examining what acts we don't perform, however, I think it might be useful to describe some of the roles that we tend to typecast ourselves in. What follows are eleven paired roles that are typically played—each role in a pair being the complement of the other.

1. *The Aristocrat* versus *The Average Guy*

The Aristocrat is perpetually proving his elegance to the world. Male *Aristocrats* love to talk about vintage wines, vintage cars, and vintage films. Their female counterparts are most familiar with Ming Dynasty vases, Louis XIV desks, and modern furniture by the likes of Florence Knoll. *Aristocrats* enjoy buying custom-tailored clothing, travel abroad with great frequency, and entertain lavishly.

They will tell you the cost of anything if you ask, but will never volunteer such costs or ask someone else what they paid for something. For to betray any preoccupation with money would mean demotion from *Aristocrat* to *Petit Bourgeois*. *Aristocrats* seem more concerned with style than substance and are, actually, stylistic trendsetters in the world of fashion.

The Average Guy, on the other hand, prides himself on being "one of the boys." He is reluctant to stand out, in any way, from his friends and neighbors for fear of being accused of "putting on airs." He will therefore say "ain't" instead of "is not," even when he prefers to use correct English. A female *Average Guy* will, if she is from a suburban working-class neighborhood, go to the beauty parlor each week and set her hair in curlers nightly. If, on the other hand, she is a sophomore at college, she will iron her hair straight and let it grow long.

The Average Guy is most fearful of being different; worried about playing *The Aristocrat* role. When asked about politics, he gives a conventional answer, conforming in all major respects to his friends' viewpoint. He sees only conventional films, reads (or only acknowledges reading) pulp fiction, and is most reluctant to ever profess an original thought or an unorthodox idea. One of *The Average Guy*'s favorite pastimes consists of poking fun at the "phoniness" of *The Aristocrat*.

2. *The Judge* versus *Humble Pie*

The Judge is the sort of person who, rather than accepting people for what they are, is always judging and morally appraising them by his own standards. Under the guise of morality, he is basically a snob. *The Judge* is intolerant of letting other people develop their own set of values, preferring to demonstrate the superiority of *The Judge*'s code of law.

The Judge is quick to tell others how to speak to people, what to say and what not to, how to protect other people's sensibilities, and what sort of behavior is "appropriate," "in-

decent," "offensive," or "acceptable." In many ways *The Judge*
represents a cross between Moses and Amy Vanderbilt.

Humble Pie, on the other hand, is a role that is based on
the biblical admonition: judge not lest ye be judged. A *Humble
Pie* person never ventures a moral or ethical position on anything. Like Episcopalians, *Humble Pie* players come in two
varieties—*High* and *Low*.

High Humble Pie-ers, when pressed for a judgment, say that
"everything is okay. It is all part of nature. There is no thing
better or worse than anything else."

Low Humble Pie-ers will respond to the same question by
pleading humility. "I'm not fit to judge such issues," they may
say. Or, "I don't know all the facts behind it."

Both *Humble Pie* positions are based on an unspoken social
contract: I won't judge you if you don't judge me. A *High
Humble Pie-er* additionally wishes to demonstrate his "enlightenment" to the world—by giving an imitation of Krishna-
murti, Gautama Buddha, or Lao-Tse. A *Low Humble Pie-er*
wishes to demonstrate his virtue through his deep humility.

3. *The Martyr* versus *I Come First*

The Martyr is a person who says, "I do, do, do for other
people. And what do they give me back? Nothing!"

While "Jewish Mothers" have been singled out as *Martyr*
types, the role is not restricted to mothers, Jews, or even
women. Many people can and do play it.

The Martyr lacks self-love and feels fulfilled only when
appreciated by others. *Martyrs* give so that others will notice
it and be grateful. And for expected future favors. When
those IOU's can't be collected, *The Martyr* puts on the big act:
"After all I've done for you, is this any way to treat me?"

At such times the skillful *Martyr* is adroit at provoking guilt in the other person. But will that satisfy *The Martyr*? "No. Because I had to *ask* him to do it for me."

I Come First is a role that not only complements *The Martyr*, but often arises as a defense to having been brought up by one. It is also true that *I Come First* can arise from having grown up on one's own—without parents to care for you. Or from having had a psychopathic parent who served as a role model.

I Come Firsters take whatever they can get, oblivious to other people's desires. They are first on line for food at parties and first around for refills. They are always asking for things that other people own—"if you don't want it any more"—or asking to borrow your car, binoculars, cigarettes, umbrella, money. As often as not, they'll return things late or "forget" to return them at all.

If you make any requests of an *I Come Firster*, you're likely to be accused of "trying to get your hooks into me—trying to control me."

An *I Come Firster* will never bring a gift when visiting friends for dinner, but expects to be given things *on those rare occasions* when he entertains others. When he does give a party, it is usually the "Bring Your Own Bottle" kind, and commences "after dinner."

4. *The Prussian General* versus *The Loyal Soldier*

The Prussian General likes to be boss. At home, *The General* barks out commands to spouse and children. At work, *The General* does likewise with those he or she supervises. Friends consist of loyal adherents who cannot seem to think for themselves or "Yes Men," looking for some secret advantage.

If you are a *Prussian General*, the chances are that you will not see yourself in such stark terms. Instead, you'd describe yourself as "the sort of person who likes to get a job done efficiently . . . a good organizer."

The General is not a very affectionate or physically touchy person, preferring instead, a grim visage and a *work* orientation. *The General* has little patience for "excuses, emotionality, cowards, or illnesses," for all conspire against efficient troop deployment.

The Loyal Soldier is a role characterized by helplessness unless there is someone around to commandeer him. *The Loyal Soldier* relies on a *Prussian General* to suggest the menu, the movie to be seen, the way to bring up children, how to dress, and what rules to abide by in the office. *Loyal Soldiers* hope to win minor promotions by serving well—but never want to reclaim the responsibility for directing their own lives. Better to leave that to the wise commanders they so patiently serve. And if things go wrong? Well, *The General* bears the biggest blame.

5. *Prim and Proper* versus *The Swinger*

The *Prim and Proper* act is a cover-up for sexual fears and/or emotional insecurity. Players are either afraid to accept their own sexual urges in general, have hang-ups regarding specific sexual practices or positions, or fear that *acting* on sexual impulses will cause a breakdown of their current life styles. This last fear refers to the fantasy that the *Prim and Proper* player could become debauched or would wreck and lose the security of home and family.

The *Prim and Proper* way to deal with these fears is *not* to acknowledge them and *not* to work against them but, instead, to couch them in terms of a superior morality and a greater virtue.

"I guess I'm just old-fashioned," a *P and P* player might retort, declining an advance from a member of the opposite sex. Or they might chill you with an "I love my husband (wife) too much to consider that," thereby implying that if *you* had any "morality" such advances would never cross your mind.

The Swingers' code is that they see sex as a cure for everything. Sex should be as casual as shaking hands. A *Swinger* "theoretician" I know went so far as to suggest that everybody should be capable of making it with everybody else. Mutual attraction isn't even necessary. Reject *The Swinger* and you'll be told that you have a "hang-up. Otherwise you'd allow yourself to turn on to me." And *The Swinger* will insist "that it is impossible for two people to know each other if they haven't been intimate."

If you accept *The Swinger*'s terms for getting to know one another "better and more intimately," you'll usually soon find him off and running, "swinging" with someone else, in another attempt to "know other people better." Most *Swingers* are putting the cart before the horse in an attempt to find a meaningful and loving relationship with someone. They have their physical intimacy *first,* before the emotional one. They then, of course, find something "missing," and so they run off to another bed for another intimacy. Over·and over and over.

6. *Women's Lib* versus *Male Chauvinist Pig*

The *Women's Lib* act is one in which the player interprets *all* of history and *all* contemporary social customs and conventions as a male "plot" against the "female race." Nothing will pass the observant eye of a *Women's Lib* actress without its being sexualized and judged—with the male always being the villain in the drama. And just as there were white liberals who, in years past, paid and applauded while being insulted by militant black lecturers, so are there some men who have adopted the *Women's Lib* act.

I am not referring here to those women who are intelligently into the Women's Liberation Movement—who can distinguish true exploitation and oppression from fantasy, and who are capable of playing other parts at other times. The *Women's Lib* act is identified more by its consistency, humorlessness, and unfairness. Such players usually do not want equality of the sexes, but seek to supplant the male in his dominant role.

I recall one incident where some *Women's Lib* types were harassing a male celebrity while he was being interviewed on television. They insulted/interrupted/threatened him for presumably not treating women as equals. On leaving the show he was still surrounded and taunted by these harpies, at which point he remarked: "If I were to treat you as equals, at this point I would punch each and every one of you in the mouth."

The *Women's Lib* actress will probably not be satisfied until the day that urinals are installed in the ladies' room of Schrafft's.

The *Male Chauvinist Pig* is the *Women's Lib* counterpart. Without him, she would be out of business. For his act is a living testament to all those stereotypical attitudes the *Women's Libber* decries.

Basically, the *Male Chauvinist Pig* is afraid of women. He refuses to see them as individual beings—as different and varied as are the men he knows. Instead he pictures them as submissive things to be dominated and screwed. Their place is "in the home," where they may look forward to "being mothers, cooks, housekeepers, and loyal wives."

The *MC Pig* is often seen putting on his act in front of his *MC Pig* friends, when he flirts, whistles at, or "talks down" to a woman. He does this in front of his companions to *prove* his doubtful male credentials to the *MC Pig* family. The woman is merely a device through which he reassures himself about his own potency.

7. *The Rebel* versus *Mr. and Ms. Maturity*

The Rebel is characterized by his stereotypical rejections of "square society." In his regularity of responses he is, of course, as predictable as the "square" he rejects. Still, he likes to think of himself as "different," "new," "independent-minded," and "in the vanguard."

Decades ago *The Rebel* came to social gatherings drunk. Now he comes stoned on marijuana. Years ago he was active in "the Workers' movement." Now he has dropped out of all movements. Long ago he argued the merits of Ionesco and Sartre. Today he argues the merits of Sunshine versus Blue Cheer "acid."

The Rebel's vocabulary is punctuated by phrases such as "boss," "far out," "groovy," "out-a-sight," "cool," "dude," and "man." The 1970s *Rebel* uniform consists of long hair, jeans, old army jackets, boots or sandals, beards for men, unshaved underarms for women, headbands, and beads.

It is considered good manners to curse a cop ("pig," in rebel parlance), put down the quality of 'work and life in the country, and apply for welfare (thus guaranteeing an income based on someone else's labor). This quite human desire to sustain oneself with minimum effort is rarely acknowledged by *The Rebel*. As far as he is concerned, he is waging "revolution" by virtue of his rhetoric, inactivity, being a public ward, and experimentation with drugs.

Mr. and Ms. Maturity's act is to put down any and all attempts at rebellion by affirming the "reasonableness" of society as it is presently constituted. They have made their own adjustment to it, are usually well off, comparatively speaking, and feel that any change in the social structure might rock the boat and threaten them. Often they have not lived through or accepted the rebellious child within themselves, and so feel uncertain about their own positions as "adults." The way they allay these fears is by playing hard at being "adult" all of the time. They talk a lot about "mature" versus "immature" behavior, about "responsibilities," and about "taking care of business." Some are into the *Law and Order* gambit. But most do no more than try to promote harmony and agreement between warring factions, just as they would expect any "grown-up" to do. They themselves are in rebellion against nothing.

There is a story told of a *Mature* rabbi who was visited by a husband complaining about his wife. After he finished, he asked the rabbi, "Who's right? Me or my wife?"

"You're right," said the soothing rabbi.

The husband left, reassured. Shortly after, the wife entered with a different version of the same story. And to the same question of "Who's right?" the rabbi told the wife: "You're right."

Now during this time, the rabbi's wife had been listening in from a back room. She charged in, after the lady left, and said, "You hypocrite. First you tell the husband he's right. Then you tell the wife she's right. You have absolutely no sense of values."

"You're right," said the rabbi.

8. *The Neurotic* versus *Anyone Can Be President*

The Neurotic unashamedly announces his fears, handicaps, anxieties, and insecurities to whoever will listen. This is particularly true if the listener has just asked *The Neurotic* to do something that the neurotic would prefer not to do. Rather than a flat-out "No," *The Neurotic* recites compelling reasons (of an emotionally crippling nature) as to *why* the task cannot be done.

"I'm scared . . . I've never done it before . . . I'm afraid of people . . . I'm afraid of failure . . . I'm afraid of getting too close . . . I'm afraid of rejection."

Neurotics are looking for good mother or father figures to watch over them, protect them, and *do for them* all of the things that they are unused to doing for themselves. Their "illness" becomes their excuse for not maturing.

While *The Neurotic* presumes that "nothing can be accomplished," the *Anyone Can Be President* act assumes anything can. All you need is hard work and diligence and anything you want is yours. *Anyone Can Be President* players make good evangelists, teachers, and social workers. They talk a lot about "hard work and effort paying off." They devise "success strategies" for every occasion, tell you how to win friends and influence people, and how to become the life of the party. While some of their recipes undoubtedly work, these players rarely allow for things such as chance, fate, and other influences beyond one's control.

9. *The Put-Down Artist* versus *The Girl Scout Cookie*

The very best *Put-Down Artists* that I have ever seen are Gore Vidal and William Buckley. Though espousing opposite points of view on most political/cultural/social matters, both are brothers beneath the skin. For they are united in their possession of waspish tongues and in the delight each seems to derive from artfully carving up someone else.

Put-Down Artists enjoy impressing others with their erudition, rhetoric, quick minds, and "superior values." And to really shine requires that they have some foil against which to operate with acerbity. The more his remarks cut another human to the bone, the more proud and pleased with himself *The Put-Down Artist* becomes. There is a lot of peacock in *The Put-Down Artist*.

The Girl Scout Cookie would *never* dream of putting anyone down. He (*The Boy Scout Cookie*) or she is interested mainly in being "good"; as wholesome and reasonable as the "girl and boy next door." Tony Randall projects the image of the *Scout Cookie*. As do Doris Day and Debbie Reynolds.

Scout Cookies have also been referred to as *Nurses' Aides* or *Red Cross Workers*. For they ceaselessly oppose *Put-Down Artists* and are always comforting the victims of other people's "attacks." Even when these victims are quite capable of verbally defending themselves.

There is a secret condescension operating in most *Girl Scout Cookies*. For they presume that others aren't capable of taking care of themselves without the "Do-Good" intervention of *The Scout Cookie*.

10. *Suzy Knickerbocker* versus *The Rock of Gibraltar*

The *Suzy Knickerbocker* role is that of a gossip columnist —passing out bits and pieces of other people's lives to third and fourth parties. It is a reportorial role that focuses on fact, rumor, and editorial opinion. A *Suzy Knickerbocker* is the equivalent of a small-town newspaper. If there is anything you want to know about anybody, ask *Suzy Knickerbocker*.

The two problems in playing this role exclusively are (a) you tend to live vicariously through other people rather than for yourself, and (b) lots of people resent your talking about them behind their backs.

I have an aunt who plays *Suzy Knickerbocker*. When I was younger, I enjoyed her company very much. She would amuse me and my family with tales told about other family members —their scandals, their fights, their outrageousnesses, their stupidities, their ludicrousness. When my aunt told these stories, it was always "in confidence," and I had the feeling that she was one of "Us," talking about "Them."

It was only later that I came to appreciate that this is the *Suzy Knickerbocker* way. And that when she was with other people, she tried to cement her relationship with *them* by bad-mouthing *us*.

The Rock of Gibraltar—otherwise known as *The Gentle Sphinx*—is *Suzy*'s opposite number. *The Rock* is steady, steadfast, and silent. You can confide in a *Rock* with great confidence, knowing that your secret will be kept.

The Rock accummulates other people's grief but never shares his or her own. That is why *Rocks* have such "strength" reputations.

The difficulty in being a *Rock* is not only that you have nobody to unburden yourself to, but you bear other people's burdens in addition.

Rocks are often lonely people and make good suicide candidates.

11. *Emily Dickinson* versus *The Life of the Party*

The *Emily Dickinson* role is that of the "super-sensitive" person. These people regularly let others know that they care about things "deeply," and are inclined to romanticize things such as loneliness, lost love, and despair. James Dean, before his death, projected such an image more skillfully than most *Emily Dickinson* types. He did it through silence and studied mood. Most *Dickinsonians* overadvertise.

They quote from plays, essays, poems, and the Bible with regularity. They treat the "problems" of life very seriously indeed, and can't very well laugh in life's face. They tend to be alarmist about man and his fate, and brood artfully.

Melancholy is a favorite *Emily Dickinson* emotion.

The Life of the Party has no such seriousness. He is always wisecracking, has a great collection of jokes (which he repeats at every party), and seems to feel comfortable only when he can entertain people and make them laugh.

Like Pagliacci, there may be a saddened heart beneath the clown's mask, but one would never guess it.

The Life of the Party has a hard time being alone—where there is no audience to appreciate his act and give him positive feedback. He suffers, unfortunately, from being a slave to someone else's smile.

The listing of roles that I have presented is by no means exhaustive. Eric Berne, in his articles and books (*Games People Play* and *What Do You Do After You Say Hello?*), has listed hundreds of acts that people have. Often we build roles around our work (*Mother, Father, Jealous Wife, Favorite Son, Housekeeper, Faithful Husband*). Or we try on other people's acts that we think are more successful than our own. Normal adolescence involves such a trying out of other's acts.

The clothes we wear are part of our act—an image we wish to project to others. Our clothes say that we are either *Rebels, Sex Kittens, Casual, Formal, Appropriate, Unconventional, Artistic,* or *Don't Give a Damn.* And just as inner changes will be reflected in ,our dress, *so will a change of costume* affect and make for inner changes. An actor, donning cape and dinner jacket, will deliver his lines differently than he would if standing in a bathing suit.

It is most important to recognize the roles you predominantly play—not necessarily to change them, but so that you can appreciate how and why other people react to you the way that they do. And it is equally important to appreciate the roles you *rarely* or *never* play. Because learning to play them is often synonymous with personal growth.

I have been impressed with how similar theatrical training is to psychotherapy. For an actor to learn to play various parts, he has to *become* that character. In doing so, he becomes more understanding not only of other people, but of all the other people who live inside of him.

The following exercises should help you become aware of role playing and get you to broaden your own performances.

EXERCISES

1. Spend the next few days watching people (old friends and new faces) from the point of view of trying to classify them according to the roles that they play. Listen to conversations between strangers on a bus, watch celebrities on television talk shows, pick up the chatter that goes on at home and/or in your office. When you listen to people, appreciate the sound and tone of their voices as well as the content.

   Make a listing of all those people close to you and write in their *Acts* next to their names—as your observations dictate.

2. Write down all of the roles you feel you play. Then write down all of those you feel you never or rarely play. Do this slowly. Allow an hour to complete this task. Finish it *before* going on to read exercise 3.

3. Each day, act out one of the roles you *don't* play *for the entire day*. See how fully you can get into this new part, and how much of yourself you can recognize in it.

4. Spend one day acting *silly*. (In this—as in all other all-day exercises—you are free to choose a workday or a weekend day.)

5. Write down the names of two of your favorite actors, stage or screen characters, or heroes. Act as each one of them would on successive days . . . and for the entire day.

6. List two actors, stage characters, or anti-heroes whom you don't like. As in exercise 5, do impersonations of them on successive days. After the work is completed, see how much of yourself you discovered in the people you played-at-being in exercises 5 and 6.

7. Following completion of exercises 1 through 6, vary your costumes for a week. If you always dress up, dress down. Do the reverse, if that is your opposite self.

   If you are a woman and dress sedately, dress sexily. If, on the other hand, you always wear miniskirts and tight-fitting sweaters, try wearing a Mother Hubbard dress.

   If you dress as a "Marlboro Man," dress more "effeminately." If a *Rebel*, dress conservatively.

   You may have to borrow or purchase some new clothes for this exercise.

11

PASSIVE AND ACTIVE

ERNEST Borgnine played the title role in a classic movie called *Marty.* In one scene he and a friend are standing around trying to decide how to pass the evening. The conversation goes approximately as follows:

"What do you want to do, Marty?"

"I dunno. Waht do you want to do?"

"I dunno. Whatever you want to do."

"Do you want to drive along the Grand Concourse and look for girls?"

"I dunno. If that's what you want to do."

"Well, whatever you want to do."

"How about going to the Loew's Paradise?"

"I dunno. If that's what you really want to do."

The conversation goes on and on and on this way. It is an excellent example of two people—neither of whom can accept *either* the passive *or* active role—trying to make a decision regarding a shared activity. Had each been capable of playing *both* roles they might have settled quickly on one choice, or decided to go driving one night and to the movies the next. Instead, they had a stalemate.

Many people are quite reluctant to actively direct things. No wonder. Their upbringing has made them self-conscious about appearing to be "pushy," "selfish," "bossy," and making "I" statements.

I remember writing compositions in public school and getting them back with the comment, "Eliminate the *I*'s." And so, instead of writing "I think people ought to be free," I began writing the categorical "People ought to be free," or the impersonal "One would think people ought to be free," or the attributive "Thoreau says that people ought to be free."

Such subtle but constant conditionings produce the Martys of the world. Or the example of Jane, who never directly says what she wants.

On a typical evening Jane will say to her husband, Ralph: "Do you feel like staying home tonight?"

If he says "Yes," he has guessed wrong, and Jane becomes more insistent in her questioning, saying something like: "We haven't been out for a week," or "It's so hot indoors."

At some point Ralph agrees that they ought to go out. Jane's next question is: "What would you like to do?"

Ralph might say, "Let's go to a movie," which is the answer Jane is waiting for. Or he may suggest that "we visit Elliot and Pam."

To the Elliot and Pam offer, Jane would counter with: "We always visit them," or "How about something else tonight?"

When Ralph suggests seeing *Goldfinger,* Jane objects that "it's too long a drive." They finally settle on *Love Story*, playing locally, which is the film that Jane wanted to see all along.

I submit that such roundabout activity bespeaks a sense of shame over being directive. It is also both a waste of time and irritating to those you are attempting to direct. A simple "I want to see *Love Story* tonight" statement can be either accepted or rejected by Ralph. In Jane's "unpushy" approach, he is liable to feel manipulated and resentful.

A person who is capable of assuming an *active* role is also one who is able to assume responsibility for his or her own life. For he is willing to direct it along the paths he chooses.

Gladys is someone unable to do that. Her attitude has always been one of resigned hopelessness. "I can't do anything about things anyway," she would say. "So why try?"

As a child, Gladys always went along with things. Some things were good. She had a few friends whom she liked and who liked her. But she felt quite unhappy with her parents' attitudes of strictness, disapproval, argumentativeness, and unaffection. Being capable of playing only a passive part, she of course said nothing.

At eighteen, she accepted the proposal of Stan, the first boy who suggested marriage. While not exactly "in love," she did like Stan and saw this as a painless way to slide out of her parents' house. Still taking no direction, she allowed herself immediately to become pregnant as she failed to assume responsibility for birth control measures.

While Gladys had no desire to have a child at nineteen years of age, she did nothing about determining the *fact* of her pregnancy until late in her third month, and never "thought" of an abortion until her fifth, when it was too late. And this was only because Stan had suggested looking into it since she seemed so unhappy.

Over the next few years, she became increasingly disaffected with Stan. He assumed no responsibility for the new child, spent many nights away from home, and was, Gladys felt, beginning to cheat on her. Yet she said nothing at all to him and continued to go along with things.

When her mother, sensing her distress, asked Gladys why she didn't leave Stan, Gladys replied: "What's the use? Do you think it would be any different with someone else?"

"Then talk to Stan," said her mother. "Let him know how you feel."

"Why?" asked Gladys. "You can't change human nature."

Learning to be passive is important. For it enables you to

"go with the flow of things." Yet, when the stream you are in doesn't suit you, it is equally essential that you *actively* pull yourself out of it and find some new stream upon which you can float.

When people *won't allow themselves* to be active, they also manage to pervert the truest meaning of passivity. For in its best sense, it means "going along with things *openly* and *receptively*." If, however, you are *unhappily* going along with things, you do it not receptively but *grudgingly* and *spitefully*. This is what psychiatrists refer to when they speak about the Passive-Aggressive Personality.

Gladys managed to display her resentfulness toward Stan in just this way. Whenever he asked her what she cared to do on any given day, her "I don't care—whatever you say" answer always implied "I don't care enough about you to either make a decision or share it with you." And she accepted his sexual advances in the same bored "let's get it over with" attitude.

If you still find yourself reacting like Gladys—unable to make choices, say what you want and what you don't want, unwilling to declare a "Yes" or a "No," this would be as good a time as any to repeat the exercises in Chapter 5.

Stuart is one who suffers from not knowing how to be passive. He runs his own business, cannot seem to delegate responsibilities, and because of this works enormously long hours. He fusses a lot over affairs at home, as well. For he presumes it necessary to check on his wife to make sure that she is attending to home/kids/social arrangements properly.

Stuart drives himself so relentlessly that he recently began showing signs of both an ulcer and high blood pressure. His doctor advised, among other things, that he take a week or two off.

Stuart had not taken a vacation in eight years—since his

children were born. His wife was delighted at the prospect of their going off to a Caribbean island and looked forward to seeing her husband "slow down." But the vacation was more aggravating to Stuart than work was. He simply could not stand taking it easy, lying on the beach, getting some sun, and "going with the flow."

People like Stuart are so busy "doing their own thing"—so insistent on directing everything and everybody about them— that they never get to savor what it's like to "take somebody else's trip," to *enjoy* being led. They are always directing activities toward projects that they already know they will enjoy. Consequently they are unable to be *led into* new experiences that they might value equally if not more.

Another aspect of passivity is *listening* to people—thereby taking both them and their message in. To listen well requires a great deal of concentration, however. It is not a "passive" pursuit in the same sense that dozing off in a hammock is.

It is surprising how many people are embarrassed by their silence. They feel it marks them as less intelligent for having little to say. Yet psychoanalysts, who are largely silent, are presumed to be wise men by their patients. And the most enlightened sages and gurus that we have are people who *rarely find it necessary to comment on anything.* Silent people may well regret their *not daring to say something* when they wish to. But they should not distort other people's perceptions of them. For in silence, they can make good and welcome listeners.

Talking is a manifestation of *activity*, and is something to be practiced, assiduously, by those who have trouble speaking to others. Yet many people overtalk. They do not use speech to communicate as much as they use it to dazzle, flatter, impress, or deceive the listener. Some talkers are so active—so in love with their own voices and so caught up in doing a verbal tap dance—that they never even seem to notice it when they've lost their audience. The listener, in this case, is simply a foil against which "The Big Talker" can do his thing.

There is an old Russian folk saying that Nikita Khrushchev was fond of quoting. It ought to be borne in mind by incessant talkers: "Better to close your mouth and have people think you are a fool than open it and prove it."

Again, I would remind you that *balance* is essential to a person in terms of activity/passivity. By that *I do not mean* that every action should be so tempered that, like *Marty*, you are left in limbo. *I do mean* that you should be capable of fully swinging either way, *without* being self-conscious over whichever role it is you are playing at any particular time.

EXERCISES

1. Find a friend, relative, spouse, or child and take a *Blind Walk* with that person. A *Blind Walk* proceeds as follows:

   One person is blindfolded and led about by the other for a full half hour. This is best done outdoors, but if that is impossible it can be done in a home or apartment. The entire procedure is to take place in silence. The "guide" is to give the blindfolded person as many things to touch/feel/experience as possible. You may brush him against things, hand him objects, introduce him to smells, roll him on the ground, and even—if trust is gained—romp freely. The *active* guide is limited solely by his imagination in this exercise. The blindfolded person is to *passively* take in as much as he or she can.

   After the half hour is up, the roles are reversed and the blindfolded person becomes the guide. Only when this is concluded are both participants free to share their experiences in leading and being led.

2. List all of the things you have done with other people during the past week. When you are finished, review the list and note whether you initiated these activities or passively went along with the other person's suggestions.

3. List those friends, relatives, and family members closest to you. With each, decide whether you are usually the initiator of activities or the follower.

4. On the basis of exercises 2 and 3, set up some specific exercises *on your own* to reverse the role you usually play with various people.

5. One morning, after arising, stand in front of a mirror, look yourself in the eye, and say aloud all of the things you want to do either that day, in the immediate future, or in the far future. These things may be petty or profound. Start each desire with the words "I want . . ." and fill in the blanks. If nothing comes to mind, continue to say "I want . . ." and *discover* what new statements come out of you.

   For the rest of that day, use the phrase "I want" as often as you possibly can in the presence of all those you come in contact with.

6. Spend two days of this week *listening* to people. *Initiate no conversations.* Respond *only when spoken to*, and do so in a way that allows the other person to go on talking.

   Don't share anecdotes or opinions unless asked to. If a person says something you are unclear about, simply get that person to elaborate.

7. Interspersed with your two days of *listening*, spend two days *talking. Initiate* all conversations with people you know and start conversations with strangers. Follow up their response with another statement. Direct conversations as much as you can and share and volunteer as many anecdotes and common experiences as you can think of.

12

ALONE AND BEING WITH PEOPLE

WHEN Herb and Gloria met, they were immediately attracted to one another. Each seemed to provide a missing element in the other's life. They saw one another constantly for six weeks, felt very much in love, and married.

Herb always considered himself to be an outsider. He felt awkward with people in general, thought of himself as a poor conversationalist, was uncomfortable in and unable to play the role of the pursuing male that "the dating game" called for.

Gloria handled her own insecurities by becoming socially gregarious. A petite, attractive, high-strung young woman, she nonetheless needed constant reassurances of her lovability. Gloria surrounded herself with people and had a large circle of friends and acquaintances. Yet she found that men constantly mistook her conversational abilities as sexual interest in them and were perpetually "pawing" her.

When they met, Gloria saw Herb as the strong, silent type —a man who could stand alone, was a good listener, and someone she could lean on. As far as Herb was concerned, Gloria "had everything." She took all the anxieties out of being with a woman, did most of the talking, and, by her social aggressiveness, determined the day-to-day activities that they embarked upon.

But their love didn't last. Because both were *looking* for qualities missing in their own personalities, they mistook the other's weakness as a *strength*. Because neither Herb nor Gloria was a complete individual, each attempted to make the other supply the characteristics that he or she lacked. Within months, a vicious cycle began to intrude upon their happiness. Herb's basic discomfort around people and Gloria's inability to be away from others proved to be an increasingly disruptive force in their relationship.

For Herb, Gloria's "conversational ability" often became "mindless chatter." Gloria, wanting to be the center of Herb's life (uncertain that she was and needing constant reassurances), was very sensitive to his slightest "turn off." Whenever she felt his silent irritation, she redoubled her chatter and demands for reassurances—all of which served to get her less and less and less. Herb, feeling more uncomfortable as their relationship suffered, became increasingly self-conscious with Gloria's friends and avoided, more and more often, Gloria's wishes to socialize.

Gloria felt trapped. She was getting less "lovability" feedback from her husband and felt resentful about Herb's unwillingness to spend time with friends and relatives. Ashamed to see other people by herself ("They would think Herb and I were having troubles") Gloria was also unable to get their reassurances about her basic decency.

Two years of this escalating cycle had left them in a relationship where resentfulness, despair, and bitterness had replaced their original ecstasy.

The ability to enjoy *both* solitude and the company of others is essential for emotional balance. Failure to appreciate either one of these states imprisons you in the other. A man who can't feel comfortable around other people—

who isolates himself from his fellows—is trapped in perpetual loneliness. A woman who can't tolerate being by herself becomes a slave to the presence of others. Neither situation is conducive to psychological health.

People who cannot stand being alone waste an enormous amount of time. They will pass countless evenings on meaningless dates, will have endless and pointless conversations with people (the *actual* point being to hold their listener next to them so that they needn't stand alone), and will stay up far too late at parties—usually being the last to leave—simply to avoid going home to an empty apartment.

Frequently they will remain with their parents far past the point of convenience, so as not to have to live alone. Or they will frustratedly tolerate unloved roommates for the same reason.

Many people have married solely to avoid living alone—or to be "rescued" from living with their parents. And once married, many husbands and wives cannot tolerate being apart for more than a few hours. When this is done out of love, it makes sense. But it is more often done out of the fearfulness of solitude. In such cases the closeness often causes resentments in the partner who can tolerate aloneness better. And it certainly limits the person who fears being alone. For he can never spend time *alone developing his own skills and interests*. Instead, he or she hangs on to a spouse as a baby hangs on to a security blanket.

This is like having a fear of the dark—except that it operates twenty-four hours a day. Persons wedded to this position *must* learn to deal with, appreciate, and even enjoy solitude. Otherwise, like Gloria, they will never develop the resources to please themselves and will always be at the mercy of others for their pleasure.

Other people are so self-conscious, so ill at ease with people, that they make themselves into virtual recluses. They tend to stay by themselves at work or at school and make a beeline for the privacy of their rooms after the day's labors are done. Dogs or cats make suitable companions for them—not people. And they spend a great deal of time substituting fantasy for company.

Around others they tend to worry about the image they project; they become aware of their own egos (instead of the egos of other people) and tend to cover up their self-consciousness with a stiff quietness that, they hope, will allow them to blend into the wallpaper.

If they could speak, they would tell you that they are quiet because they worry, as Herb did, over saying the "right thing" (whatever that is), or that they have nothing to say. It never seems to occur to them that they could simply say what they are *feeling* or what they are *thinking*. Or that the world loves a good listener.

Such people tend to brood a great deal and feel sorry for themselves. Occasionally they may romanticize their role as "the loner." But this gives them little permanent comfort.

There are, finally, those who can tolerate neither solitude nor being with people. Wherever they are they would rather be someplace else. When they are in the company of others, their discomfort is such that they want to be alone. But shortly after being alone, their loneliness impels them to seek out company.

James Thurber told a story of a rabbit standing in the middle of the road as a car approached. Thinking of fleeing to safety, the rabbit hopped on his right foot, planning to run off in that direction. But no sooner did he put his right foot down, when he thought that it would be better to flee to the left side of the road. And so he hopped back to his left foot. This uncertainty kept repeating itself as our rabbit kept hopping from side to side . . . left/right/left/right. He was finally run over by the car.

People who can't take either aloneness or company are the worst off of all. Like the rabbit, they are run over by life. Rather than deal with the situation they are in—rather than act counterphobically—they are perpetually fleeing to a "comfort" that doesn't exist.

When I was a young man I had my own difficulties in being alone. I was particularly "embarrassed" to do *public* things alone such as eating in a restaurant or going to a movie. I was worried about other people watching me, fearful that I would stand out for being alone. I would anticipate hearing them whisper about me, "How come that young man is all by himself? Doesn't he have *any* friends?"

This concern with my *image* caused me, on innumerable occasions, to either sit at the counter of a cheap diner, buy a sandwich at a local grocery that I might eat while walking on the street, or prepare my own meal at home when what I really wanted was to go to a Chinese restaurant for a feast.

One day, in my own counterphobic way, I willed myself to confront this fear and walked into a restaurant at noontime. I was seated at a table by myself, and ordered.

After a drink, I looked up and discovered that nobody was interested in me. Those in company were talking to one another. And those others eating alone usually had their heads buried in a book or a newspaper.

I repeated this process a few more times and the self-consciousness finally left. I discovered, in the process, that when I feared being looked at, all I had to do was look at and observe others to make my unreasonable self-consciousness go away. And I also appreciated my irrational *symbolism*—namely, that being by myself meant that I was unlovable and unacceptable. It was no longer necessary, understanding this, to continue to deny the obvious fact of my moments of aloneness.

One sees the same process in young women or men who want to go to a dance, a meeting, a museum, or a singles bar *but won't go unless they can get a friend to accompany them.* They need a public manifestation of their friend to publicly affirm the fact that they are not desperate—that they are lovable. As if going alone really meant those things. And when they can't get a friend to accompany them, they miss out.

Even when they do find a friend willing to join them in going to a place where they might meet and be with new people, they seem to be impelled to go to great lengths to deny that that is why they are there.

"I came because my girlfriend wanted to come . . . I live in the neighborhood and thought I'd drop by . . . I had a date but he didn't show up, and having nothing better to do, I thought I'd come here," they might say.

Or better yet, "I'm looking for an old friend" (who, of course, was never supposed to be there).

Then they go on to criticize all the "poor desperate people around here," as though putting down others could add to their self-respect. Or as if it were a sin to try to meet new people.

The exercises that follow are geared toward helping you appreciate aloneness and company—unashamedly. Providing, that is, that you are willing to act counterphobically. To be able to be productively alone will also enable you to bring more to a relationship with others. For you will then have your own private moments and interests to share with and stimulate others.

EXERCISES

1. Make a list of places where you go only when accompanied by someone.
   Go to each of these places alone.

2. List those activities that you invariably perform alone.
   Invite someone to share these activities with you.

3. Fantasize where you would go on an ideal date. Then make a date with *yourself* and go to these places alone.

4. Spend two nights this week by yourself. Carefully plan these evenings so that you can give yourself maximum pampering/ stimulation/pleasure. (Don't spend the night in front of your television set eating a precooked dinner.)

5. Spend two nights this week in the company of others. Go places where people talk to one another. Spend one of these nights with friends or acquaintances and another with strangers (at a political or social club, in a bar, or at a dance or party).

6. Eat alone in an elegant restaurant.

7. Throw a dinner party at your home.

8. If you are the type of married person whose life *is not* independent of your spouse's:
   (a) Find some regular weekend or weeknight activity (golf, tennis, ceramics, political or social project, card game, museum touring, film- or theater-going) that you can partake of *alone* (without your mate).
   (b) For the next month, try to make as many household and personal decisions as you can *alone* (by consulting yourself instead of your partner, parents, friends).
   (c) Spend one day each week for four consecutive weeks pretending that you are alone—with neither spouse nor children. Work on relating to other men and women that day strictly in terms of an "I-they" relationship. Don't

bring up your own family in conversations with others. Discover, instead, what else you might discuss or do.

9. Take a weekend vacation by yourself.

10. Take a weekend vacation *with* someone (friend, acquaintance, relative, or mate).

13

WORK

IT is most important that we consider the influence of work upon a person's emotional well-being. Men and women who enjoy their work have much more vitality than those who don't. When a person works at a job he dislikes or is bored by, he becomes both drained and irritable.

Performing a job that is meaningless and distasteful to you is much like serving a half-time jail sentence. After all, you sleep eight hours a day. Of your sixteen hours of wakefulness, you thus spend half of them in tedium, counting the minutes until the day ends—much as a convicted felon counts the days until his time is up.

Quitting a distasteful job and doing *nothing* is not the answer either. Not unless you have saved enough money to support yourself. For without a job you will have to rely on someone else for support. That someone else will be either a parent, spouse, or the local welfare office. The difficulty with that arrangement (whatever the short-term advantages are) is that your self-esteem will erode in subtle yet definite ways.

Either you will begin to resent the person subsidizing you or that person will begin to resent you. You will compare yourself to other people on the welfare rolls and know, somewhere deep down inside, that you are a fraud—that you could do some form of work if you made the effort. One pays a price for everything in life. And the cost to you of deriving your income from someone else's labors is in the loss of self-respect.

In my psychiatric practice I have seen many young people making the "East Village hippie scene" who have finagled themselves onto the welfare rolls. At first they are pleased with their new-found leisure and income. But shortly afterward decay sets in. They either begin sleeping their days away, fill up their empty time with meaningless "hanging around" and drugs, or take jobs "off the books" to supplement their welfare payments—thereby turning themselves into deceivers.

To value oneself, a person *can't* be a cheat and *must* earn his own daily bread. All wise men have recognized this principle. In a Buddhist lamasery, a day of no work is a day of no food.

If you are working at a job you enjoy (which includes being a *contented* housewife), or if you are at school, preparing for a *desired* job, this chapter does not apply to you, and you might just as well go on to Chapter 14. However, if you are *not* feeling fulfilled on your job or at school it is important not only to consider the reasons for your dissatisfaction, but to see what can be done to change things.

Some people create job problems for themselves because they are unable to delegate responsibilities. They insist on performing as many tasks as are humanly possible, usually do the work of two or three people, *and if* they have employees under them they insist upon checking up on the work of their underlings.

These "nondelegators of responsibility" assume that they and they alone are competent workers and that everybody else is a "fuck-up." They either surround themselves with incompetents (the better to prove their own indispensability) or more likely undercut their subordinates' initiative by perpetually checking up on them and doing their work for them. For subordinates (like everyone else) learn only through their mistakes. "The Super-Responsible Person" doesn't allow them to learn because he is unwilling to allow them to make their own mistakes.

Many self-employed people suffer from this inability to delegate some of their work to others. So do many housewives, who never involve their kids or husbands in helping with chores "because they couldn't do them as well as I can."

Perhaps you find your job tedious/boring/unstimulating/ distasteful. You would like to do something else but you don't. You tell yourself that it would require too great an effort. You would lose income, or have to go back to school. Or you convince yourself that you'd find any job boring after a while.

All the above reasons may well be true, but they are also all cop-outs. For there is no reason you couldn't be enjoying your work instead of dreading it, as any careful examination of the above excuses will show.

It's Too Great an Effort. This excuse is one of the most shortsighted ones imaginable. It is true that changing jobs might require a great deal of work or effort. The beginner would have to put some time into thinking about alternatives. You'd have to make lists of what tasks you like to do and what you don't; what skills you have and what you'd need to acquire. You'd have to let your imagination roam in thinking of other potential jobs. You might want to research the requirements of these other jobs. This would mean making phone calls to various schools, professional organizations, union offices, state licensing offices, or potential employers. It might even mean making an appointment to see a vocational counselor.

You may, after all of this, discover you need to make some

hours available for additional training. Or even have to try out the "new job" for a while to see if you like it any better than your current one. So it is, I concede, a big effort.

And yet the average working person spends two thousand hours a year at his job. To my way of thinking, *it is a greater effort to force yourself to do something distasteful for two thousand hours than it is to spend from forty to a hundred hours considering how to change it.*

I would lose income. Switching jobs often causes a loss of income. This may be temporary (if you have to attend school for training purposes or start a business of your own) or permanent (jobs that pay greater satisfactions might also pay less money). This shouldn't really be a problem. Most of us can live on far less than we earn right now. We only think that we can't. That's because we tend to confuse our *possessions* with *ourselves.*

Can you remember back to a time when your income was less than a third of what it is today? Yet you seemed to enjoy life just as much then, and likely had more free time to boot?

What happens is that we get caught up in the materialistic treadmill. We buy cars, homes, appliances, clothes, furniture, and other assorted gewgaws. And we have to work longer and harder *to support these contrivances*—not ourselves. Eventually we find not only precious little time to enjoy our worldly goods but also that we're trapped into keeping a tedious job in order to maintain them.

Many husbands find themselves in such situations. Their wives have been raising children and are now suburban housewives. One way out of this trap is to talk to your wife about your desire to try something else and see whether or not she might be able to take on a job to compensate for the income you would lose.

The other way out of the materialistic trap is just to drop

out of it. Sell the car. Move into a cheaper home. Wear blue jeans and corduroys instead of tailored suits. It can be done. Unless, of course, you feel that your trappings are more important to you than getting out of your work trap is.

I'd have to go back to school. I've heard this excuse offered many times for failure to shift careers. It is a particularly popular one among *bored* housewives. Their complaint is that they never liked school when they were younger and/or didn't do very well academically. What they fail to appreciate is that at thirty-four years of age they'd *have a purpose* in attending school. When they were youngsters they simply went out of habit. This *motivation*, plus the additional wisdom gained during the ten to twenty years since they left school, would be more than enough to see them through.

I'd find any job boring after a while. This is the lamest excuse of all. First, you don't *really* know that. Second, even if you do find that your new job *eventually* bores you, what would prevent you from trying a third, fourth, or fifth job?

Things are usually most interesting *when we are learning something new.* When we have mastered one job, we are naturally curious to test ourselves against something new. We require new stimulation and new knowledge to keep our interests up. Some jobs provide for this. Others don't. If we force ourselves to keep working at something we *no longer have to think about*, we perform like machines.

I worked as a prison psychiatrist for three years. During the first year it was extremely interesting to me. I had an opportunity to meet and understand the attitudes of people I would never have ordinarily come into contact with.

In the second year my interest came from trying to develop new programs that might make for more effective rehabilitation.

By the third year it became apparent that the bureaucrats

who run the New York City prisons would not accept any
fundamental changes in their nonrehabilitative "rehabilitation
program." And I felt that I had learned all I possibly could
about criminality—its causes, attitudes, and possible cures.

Work became a bore in that third year. I could neither
apply what I knew in new ways nor tolerate the repetitiveness
of what I was hearing or doing. So I quit a $15,000 a year
position rather than continue to go in late, watch the clock,
and leave early. I felt that *anything* else I could find to do in
the future would be more interesting and rewarding to me.
In my value system, money does not compensate for monotony.

Many others apparently share my feelings. For it is becoming increasingly popular for people to change career lines in
their thirties and forties. More and more people are unwilling
to settle for the idea of one life/one job—particularly when
they have outgrown jobs that initially interested them.

The psychoanalyst I saw when I was twenty-four was such
a woman. The mother of four children, she lived with a man
who was able to support her quite nicely. Approaching forty,
with her children no longer requiring full-time mothering, she
applied to medical school, was accepted, and from there went
into psychiatry.

Joe, a neighbor on the block where I grew up, had
had a successful yarn business. On weekends and vacations
he spent a great deal of time fishing and lobstering. He, his
sons, and his wife loved boats and the sea. In his mid-forties
he sold his business and began a career as a commercial
fisherman.

My wife is a professional actress. She and a friend of hers
were sitting about one day lamenting all of the "bull" you have
to put up with to get into a show. And about the financial
insecurity of the acting profession. Her friend had once seen

a production put on by psychiatric patients at Austin-Riggs Hospital. They both thought that they would enjoy working with such people. So they *created* new jobs for themselves by going, at first, to the Mount Sinai psychiatric clinic as volunteers—using theater techniques with patients. Their program was so popular that they applied, successfully, for funding.

Frank was a banker and later a government economist. In his late thirties he became interested in psychological groups because of experiences he had in attending Gestalt Therapy groups. He also began to appreciate how meaningless his own work had become to him. One day he liquidated his assets, quit his job, and put a down payment on an old farm house. He contacted a number of Encounter centers and offered to rent them this facility for weekend and week-long groups. He found his involvements with people as a psychological inn-keeper much more rewarding than his previous office work. With additional training, he eventually began to lead his own groups as well.

Bob worked in the music industry, for a firm that promoted record albums. A man who had some design background, he also had his own ideas about how to package records so as to sell them more effectively. He made it a point, while employed, to learn all aspects of the business—many of which had nothing to do with his own job. He learned what an album cover should cost, where the raw materials were bought, and who the printers were. Eventually he quit his position and established his own business—designing and packaging album covers.

I am sure that you can also think of people who have changed jobs and modified their career lines because of dissatisfactions with their previous work. Some jobs are *innately* boring. I think particularly of assembly-line work at factories. You may need a job like that temporarily, to pay the rent. But unless you can see yourself being promoted out of it in the near future, you might consider other alternatives.

Many other jobs are not inherently boring—even though many people become bored in them. We have all seen the bus driver, taxicab driver, housekeeper, housepainter, gardener, maintenance man, housewife, or cop on the beat who really enjoys his or her work. They have a good word for everyone and take pride in their performances. We are, unfortunately, a society more concerned with getting a job finished than we are with the quality of the job itself. *Those who enjoy their work are enjoying the here and now of the work process. Those who are disgruntled are looking to have the process completed.* And you can *never* get *into* your job if you are only waiting for it to be over and done with.

An ideal job would be one in which you not only do (or *create*) the work that you like to do, but also one in which you *work with people that you like.* This is an area too often unexplored. What it requires is discussing with your friends the possibilities of working with them or working at something entirely new—by pooling your talents and assets. Building something with someone you care about—sharing work with that person—can often provide great satisfaction and meaning where the job, in and of itself, might not.

The exercises in this chapter will help you rethink your work situation. What you then do about it, of course, is up to you. Before proceeding with these tasks, however, I would like to comment on the student's place of work—school.

The problem for many students is that school has lost its relevance. The purpose of an education has been, traditionally, to teach the three R's—reading, 'riting, and 'rithmetic—

and to prepare a person for an occupation. Along the way, our educational system has taken over many functions never intended for it. It is expected to perform babysitting functions (witness the number of pre-school programs, after-school programs, and the authorities' insistence on keeping rebellious students in classes *when they don't want to be there*), disciplinary functions, and amorphously vague educational functions—as indicated by the overabundance of "academic" university programs and the public's insistence that everyone have a college education.

For what? Most college programs leave a graduate as fit or unfit to work as does a high school diploma. Some students do settle on a career line at college (law, medicine, physics, chemistry) but then have to go on to graduate school to get any real training in these fields. Others use their undergraduate training to gain a job skill (as teachers, architects, etc.). But far too many people use universities as a place to find a spouse, postpone working, gain initials to add to their names, or satisfy their parents who insist that their children have a college degree. No wonder so many students do drop out and so many others think about it.

It is this question of *whether or not to drop out* that troubles many students that I have seen. They are torn, often, between having no sense of direction about where their education is leading them, and at the same time feeling guilt for being failures or cop-out artists when they consider leaving school.

I would think that by the time a student is midway through his second year at college, he or she ought to have *a definite idea* of what specific occupation his education is preparing him for. And if he doesn't—or if he doesn't really look forward to doing that type of work—he most definitely *ought* to drop out of school and into a job.

One usually learns far more about work from on-the-job training than by spending time in a college classroom. And if, after working a while, you decide that you want to go into a field that requires further education, *there is nothing in the world preventing you from returning.* When you have a goal, you will be much more motivated to learn. School, this second time around, will cease to be a drag—something you want to see "over with"—and instead become an active, alive process that you will enjoy taking part in.

To stay at school when it has no point for you—when it is a tedious bore—makes no more sense than staying at a pointless, boring job after giving it a fair trial. You'd be better off following your instincts to change course than trying to live up to an *image* of yourself as a "college grad" (whatever good *that* does you) or to your parents' expectations. If you feel a loss of face, a fear of disappointing others, that is what you should deal with counterphobically—not your tedium.

EXERCISES

1. List those work tasks that you perform alone and feel yourself to be quite competent in. For the next week, try delegating these responsibilities to others.

2. Allow yourself a full half-hour fantasy in which you imagine that you quit your current job within the week. Fantasize what happens to you next. Whom do you first tell of your leaving? What is their response? How does it affect those around you? What impact will it have in a week? In a month? What becomes of your current living arrangements? What do you do next with your life? Project yourself as far into the future with this fantasy as you can. At the same time, pay attention to all the small details of this future life.

3. On a sheet of paper, list in one column all of your skills and interests. In another column write down all of the tasks you currently perform that you don't have any great aptitude for or don't enjoy.

    Show these columns to three respected friends/teachers/family members, and ask them what sort of occupations might fulfill your *interest* list and avoid your *displeasure* list.

4. Spend one day performing your current tasks from a new point of view. Instead of rushing to get your tasks *over with*, see how fully you can get into experiencing them anew.

    If your work consists of washing dishes, appreciate the smell of the soap, the feel and temperature of the water, the weight of the dishes, and their transformation when washed. If doing office work, pretend you are doing your tasks for the very first time.

    See how fully you can get into *choreographing* every aspect of your work—trying to experience it as a dance instead of an ordeal.

5. Have three different fantasies in which you have no obligations and are freed of all those people you currently know or live with. You can be and do anything you wish. When you have finished, list the various occupations you chose.

6. Spend time researching the specific requirements of all those occupations listed in exercise 5. Discover where one would learn this occupation, where one applies for a job, what the prerequisites are, the salaries paid, and what opportunities there are for advancement in each.

7. List two or three people you are fondest of and, with each of them, discuss ways in which you might work together.

14

GIVING AND RECEIVING

WHEN I was a young boy, I had a neighbor who baked delicious cookies. Whenever there was a fresh batch, she invited a group of us kids over for samples. We each received a handful of tollhouse or chocolate chip delights which we munched down hungrily, along with a glass of cool milk. When we were finished our hostess would ask, "Who would like some more?"

As much as I wanted a second helping, I would say "No, thank you" after my first. For I had been taught to be "polite."

Politeness presumed that the cookie giver was not sincere in offering us more—that she was really fearful about having us children eat her out of house and home—but felt "obliged," by politeness, to offer seconds.

Politeness also meant that I, the cookie taker, should lie, saying "No, thanks," when I really wanted to say "Yes, please."

Now this is truly an absurd situation. I can appreciate, as an adult, that this woman *liked* to feed and treat children. I didn't have to "protect her" from her own generosity. I was setting myself up in the position of *presuming to read her mind and know her best interest more than she herself did.* What arrogance. Yet I see the same scenario played out daily by many adults.

My neighbor had no problem in giving, but I surely developed one in receiving. *Even if she was insincere about her offer to give*, I should have been able to say "Yes, thank you." Why? Because if her offer was accepted often enough and if she actually resented handing out dozens of cookies, *she would eventually have had to get herself together so as to stop making phony offers*.

To praise or give something to others simply because you enjoy them, enjoy pleasing them, or want to demonstrate your love is a very rewarding experience. It is equally satisfying to receive favors or compliments with a clear conscience and an appreciative "thank you" instead of the protestations we so often hear.

To learn how to give sincerely requires, first, that we examine our *insincere* motivations for giving. This means looking at the hidden agendas behind the compliments and gifts we hand to others.

Jeanette, whom I met at prison, used to crochet mufflers, hats, and skirts for her sister inmates. She gave these gifts "because I like to make things and give them to people I like." One day Jeanette was upset and wanted to talk to someone. The first person she approached had something else she wanted to do at the moment. "Generous" Jeanette was furious/pouty/hurt/insulted. She felt that her friend was disloyal—and that in view of the gifts she had given her, her friend was "obligated" to respond affirmatively the first time Jeanette called upon her.

Ellen is someone with sexual problems. She has never enjoyed the act and "tolerates" it only when necessary. Her husband, George, perpetually brings her small favors while, at the same time, acting "hurt" for being physically rejected. His underlying motives? To shame his wife—through his "hurtness" and "generosity"—into being more available to him.

Jack is another fellow who showers his wife with gifts and flattery. He often comes home with flowers, clothing, perfume, records, antiques, or jewelry to show his wife "what a wonderful gal I think you are." His hidden reason? To ease his conscience over having extramarital affairs.

I, in the past, found myself giving gifts to my former wife simply to appease her when she was angry over something. Another man I know gives gifts to his wife as "protection money," to insure her even-temperedness in advance.

Roberta never forgets to send a small gift to relatives on their birthdays. The rest of the year she is an extremely inhospitable woman. This birthday remembrance is her way of denying and doing yearly atonement for her basic "ungivingness."

Mimi pretends that she is *giving* herself sexually to her boyfriends. She refuses to see a sexual relationship as one in which *two people agree to take from each other*. And so she feels hurt and unfairly treated when her boyfriends don't spend a great deal of money on her and don't propose marriage "after all I gave them."

Helen, an elderly woman, gives things away to everybody: gifts, her own possessions, greeting cards, money. In her case, giving things away sustains the illusion that she has close friends. In actuality, most of those who know her think of her as an eccentric.

Other people never give. They are reluctant to give compliments for fear of letting the other person know how much they like him. And they are certainly not into giving gifts. For they are trying to sustain an image as totally self-sufficient people. They fear that giving to others will impoverish, rather than enrich them. If that is your problem, there is no solution other than tackling the problem directly: *by attempting to share with others things you like about them* and doing and/or giving them small favors.

Phrases such as "You shouldn't have . . . I don't deserve it . . . It embarrasses me . . . No, thank you," are often mouthed by people who have trouble receiving. Otherwise a "thank you," a smile, or a warm embrace would be more in order.

You might have difficulty receiving, as I did, because you *presume yourself to be responsible for the other fellow's generosity.*

Or because you don't consider yourself to be the sort of person who *deserves* nice things. Well, that's *your* opinion. If you want to maintain that fiction, it is certainly your prerogative to do so. But it's the *other* person's opinion that results in your getting something. Who are you to tell him that his opinions are not as valid, for him, as yours are for you?

Others are embarrassed when given things because *the thing they are given conforms with their secret desires about the other person.* They feel ashamed of these desires and worried that the giver might "read them" correctly. They then suspect that others' kindnesses are "insincere" or "given out of pity." This is a most unenviable position to be caught in—wanting something and then refusing to accept what you most want.

There are, finally, those who are so fearful of being disappointed that they try to show the world that they want nothing from anybody. To receive something gratefully would show a chink in their armor—that they might *care.* Caring makes them vulnerable only if newly expressed needs aren't met. The *Not Caring* act is their way of preventing disappointment. What such people don't appreciate is that such closedoffness also prevents them from ever finding satisfactions.

The greatest gift you can give another person (or receive from him) is total acceptance and total honesty. Totally accepting someone means *not expecting him to be any different than he is*. If you offer total honesty as well, *he will always know where he stands with you*.

The exercises that follow not only consist of practicing the arts of giving and receiving; they ask you to examine some of your present-day motivations behind these acts. *I do not want you to judge these motivations too harshly, however*.

Most of the individual things we do have dozens of underlying motivations. If you flatter people or give them gifts it may be because *you want your favors returned as well as wanting to show them that you like them*. There is nothing "evil" about such mixed motivations. That's just where you are right now. If you can accept these mixed motivations and if you can *reason yourself out of expecting something back*, that is more than sufficient.

EXERCISES

1. List the things you have given to people in the past month. Also list the compliments you've paid people this past week.

   Once the list is completed, examine each listing and see if you can discover hidden motives behind your gifts.

2. Write down all the critical judgments you have about your mate, parents, children, friends.

   Examine the list when you are finished and see whether you can devise your own exercises so as to be able to offer greater acceptance to these people. (You might try *being* them—via encounters with empty chairs—try to impersonate and share in their "foibles," grant them the right to be different than you, refer to the exercises in Chapter 3—or do anything else you can think of.)

   If you find there is little you can accept about certain people you are close to, you ought to reevaluate why you continue your relationship.

3. Recall all of your activities during the past twenty-four hours. List, particularly, all of the good feelings you had for others or the good thoughts you had about them. Notice what percent of the time you *told* the other people of your good feelings about them.

4. For the next week, work studiously at saying a simple "thank you" whenever you are complimented or receive a favor.

5. List all of the things that you like and appreciate about each of your friends and relatives. Over the next week make it a point to tell each of them of your feelings.

6. List anywhere from three to five of your favorite people. Give each of them some small gift as a token of your love.

15

FRIENDS AND STRANGERS

I'll get by with a little help from my friends.
The Beatles, from *Sgt. Pepper's
Lonely Hearts Club Band*

THERE is an oft-quoted but rarely appreciated biblical phrase, "Do unto others as you would have others do unto you." People who abide by this code are not likely to need my counsel concerning how to make acquaintances of strangers and how to turn acquaintances into friends.

Beyond a few elaborations on the above quotation, I do not feel it necessary to spend a great deal of time discussing the subject of friends and strangers. For I believe that if you have worked conscientiously on mastering all of the preceding chapters in this book, friendships with some and casual acquaintances with others will follow much as day follows night.

Those who miss out in their relationships with people usually do so because of a failure to put themselves in the other person's shoes (either that or they sequester themselves in their rooms—out of other people's sight). In my adolescence and young adulthood there were many instances when I wanted to be *invited* to do things by other people, *included* in their plans, *treated warmly*, and *told flattering things* by them. And yet, as I look back, I see that I rarely offered these same things to others. No wonder, then, that others *rarely* gave me what I wanted.

As a youth I felt that *only I* was insecure. In good part that was because I didn't dare *share* my self-doubts with others. I didn't want to reveal myself to be the only flawed person in the world.

As an adult who has shared these and other feelings, I've come to appreciate the big illusion I was operating under— the "joke" I was playing on myself. The *illusion* was that people are fundamentally different. The actuality is that the *you* in you is similar to the *me* in me.

I realize now that what I experienced as my peers' "aloofness and uncaringness" in my teen-age years was *a manifestation of their insecurities and discomforts around people*. It had nothing to do directly with *me*. Not only that, but my "real" insecurities and self-doubts were mistakenly interpreted by others as the same "aloofness and uncaringness" I was silently accusing them of.

What a trick to play on myself. What a hoax. What a waste of time and suffering.

And yet, how many of you still play that game on yourselves? When you walk into a room full of strangers, do you put them at ease? Or do you expect *them* to do that for *you*.

When you are introduced to someone, do you worry that he is judging you? Have you considered, even for a moment, that he might worry that you are judging him?

When you are with a friend and feel "disturbed vibrations" between the two of you, do you ever feel that your friend may not be telling you something he feels? Has it occurred to you that your friend might be thinking the same thought? Will you honestly tell your friend that this is on your mind? Or will you expect him to take the initiative?

The important thing to remember around strangers or people you have just met is that they often feel as strange around you as you do around them. And if you can stop watching your own *dis*-ease and, instead, put the stranger at ease, in the "doing" your own discomfort will end.

How do you put people at ease? How do you get others to take you into their confidence and establish meaningful friendships? The answer is simple. You take them into *your* confidence and share *your* thoughts, feelings, foibles, and private events with them.

I firmly believe that the reason many troubled and lonely people don't have friends is that they don't appreciate the above principle. And why should they? Most of the psychotherapists that they see don't seem to realize it either.

When I received my formal psychiatric and psychoanalytic training not a word was mentioned about this self-evident fact. Not only that, but I was instructed to keep my private life a secret. It was presumed that this was "good" for the patient; that telling him of myself would only confuse him and cause him to modify what he would tell me.

Imagine my surprise when I attended a marathon Encounter session* led by Dr. Albert Ellis some years back. When people in his group would, on occasion, ask him about personal and intimate details of his life, he had the daring to fully answer their questions. And what happened? His "patients" then revealed details about their lives that they had heretofore been too embarrassed to offer.

I appreciated, at that moment, that I had modified and limited my patients' verbal productions by my *anonymity*. When I dared reveal myself to them, they were likely to reveal themselves to me. In short, I realized that contrary to "professional opinion," psychiatrists have to practice the "openness" that they preach.

Since that day of awakening, I have had repeated confirma-

* A marathon session is a group that runs, uninterruptedly, for from twelve to twenty-four hours.

tions of this principle: if you reveal yourself to others, they will reveal themselves to you. This "sharing" is what interpersonal closeness is all about. You can readily prove this lesson to yourself any time you care to try it.

I recall the late comedian Lenny Bruce giving a performance in a movie theater. There were about two thousand people present. At one point he got onto a routine about the secrecy precautions he took and shame he left about urinating in a sink. As he said this, one thousand men—half the audience—laughed in recognition of seeing themselves. Strangers, moments ago, they all looked around at the other laughing male faces and, seeing and sharing this "secret" with one another, laughed all the more heartily. All of us in the audience were closer for that moment.

One of the reasons that I wrote my autobiography, *A Psychiatrist's Head*, was to practice what I preach: that there are no such things as secrets, that there is nothing to be ashamed of, that a full revelation of self makes others share more with you. In that book I forced myself to report on the most intimate details of my personal and private life—details that I previously would have considered "embarrassing." The effect this sharing had on me confirmed my convictions. For in the public telling, what minor shame I had experienced vanished. Also, people I hadn't known too well who read the book suddenly began sharing with me similar "secrets" in their own lives.

"So far you've been addressing yourself to people who don't make friends because they isolate themselves," I can hear my editor saying. "What about those people who are excessively friendly? People who talk and reveal themselves to others ad nauseam?"

We have all known such people. Perhaps you are one of

them. I think that such "excessively friendly types"—such "overtalkers"—have never conquered the problems of *learning to enjoy passivity* (Chapter 11) and *learning to enjoy solitude* (Chapter 12). Their hyperactivity with others is a manifestation of their fear of being alone and/or being quiet and going with the flow. These states must be mastered if such people are to establish genuine friendships.

To repeat, then. The rule for making and deepening friendships is to *treat others in the way you wish them to treat you.* This must include being honest with them, for I am sure you want that in return.

Do you feel you get as good as you give with your friends? Do they entertain you as much as you entertain them? Can you say "No" to them? Would you tell them if you had feelings that your dealings with one another were not reciprocal? I would hope so. Because if you couldn't do that safely, there is not much value to be placed on the friendship. Better to call it an acquaintanceship instead.

And if you follow these rules, will you then be *guaranteed* deep friendships with all acquaintances and good acquaintanceships with strangers? Of course not. These rules only provide you with a *structure* that *will allow friendships and acquaintanceships to develop if both parties have mutual interests.* These principles will prevent you from *missing out* on a "could-have-been" friendship. If adhered to they will prevent you from tripping over your own feet.

Friendships, like marriages, require a complex *nonanalyzable* bond between people—"chemistry," as the popular idiom has it. There are many people you could never be friendly with. Either they have other demands on their time and, "no hard feelings," literally *don't have time* for you, or they are on "bum trips"—arrogant, defensive, aloof, overly shy, cruel.

If you have worked on making yourself into an accepting person, *you will accept these others as the strangers they wish to be.* And, rather than getting hung up on trying to make someone a friend who doesn't wish to be one, you will clear the decks, emotionally, and allow friendships to develop with some of those who desire you.

EXERCISES

1. List the ways in which you would like to be approached by an "ideal" stranger.

2. Approach someone you either don't know or have just met in the ways you have listed in exercise 1. If your experience is not a successful one, keep repeating it until you have success.

3. Think of an admired acquaintance. What would you wish that person to say, do, or offer, so as to have a closer relationship together?

4. Come on to the person you thought of in exercise 3 in the way you would like that person to come on to you.

5. Approach another acquaintance in the same way.

6. For the next week, make it a point, whenever *you* feel discomfort, *to notice* the person or persons you are with and see if *they* are uncomfortable.

7. If your discomfort with someone persists, *tell that person* or persons of your dis-ease. You needn't have a *reason* for it at your fingertips. They might even suggest a reason for it.

8. Spend the next few days looking at people anew. See if you can notice the number of people who seem to like and admire you—people you never noticed before or took for granted *when you were focused on noticing people who didn't like you all that much.*

16

DEATH

To be born twice is no more amazing than to be born once.

DEATH as a subject of concern has largely been ignored by psychologists and psychiatrists alike. In this, the mental health professionals are not unlike many other of our citizens who prefer not to deal with the issue—who go about their lives acting as if death were nonexistent. I believe that such an attitude does people a great disservice, because understanding, accepting, and appreciating death are essential in order to appreciate and fully live one's life.

Perhaps a majority of our population lives in fear of death. This fear is handled by either avoiding the issue entirely or living in great dread of one's eventual demise—as exemplified by hypochondriacal symptoms, many phobic conditions (fear of flying, elevators, high places, the dark) or suicidal preoccupations (picking *your* time to end life rather than go through the anxieties of leaving the timing to fate).

We send our dying relatives off to hospitals where they can pass on out of our sight, attached to tubes, IV's, resuscitators, suction devices, and oxygen tents by physicians who consider it a personal failure to allow people to die quietly, with dignity, and without their radical interventions. We have a great aversion to seeing dead bodies and, traditionally, cover them with

161

sheets when the last breath has expired. If you walk into a room where a woman or a man is dying, you are likely to find that most people stand or sit at arm's length from the dying one—as if death, like some virus, will rub off and kill them, too.

Yet death can't be avoided—no matter how hard we try. At some point death will descend on each and every one of us. At that moment of truth, one can't look the other way. Those who have prepared themselves well will not panic at that time, but will take death's ride wherever it leads.

Why is it that we stand in such fear of death? People in other cultures don't necessarily share our terror. "For the Easterner," one Japanese survivor of Hiroshima said, "death is not seen as a finality but, like birth, simply another door through which we must pass."

Many Orientals accept death better than we do because they have been taught to do so by the society they live in. Our culture, by the same token, teaches us that death is to be considered a feared antagonist.

Newsweek magazine, May 1, 1972, had a cover showing a young man in pain on a hospital bed, an oxygen mask over his face, and a headline "HEART ATTACK—Curbing The Killer." That death is the enemy is a message thrown at us subtly yet constantly in books, magazines, film, television, and radio. Deaths constitute "news" (births, of course, rarely do). Our "scientific" way of thinking perpetuates the idea that with research and proper funding, all ills can be overcome. Cancer *will* and *should* be conquered, heart disease *will* and *should* be eliminated, tuberculosis *will* and *should* disappear, automobiles *can* and *should* be made safe enough to avoid all fatalities, famine *can* be avoided—along with plagues, war, and environmental pollution. Both semen and freshly expired people are being frozen in attempts to preserve them until that golden day when technology conquers nature. In short, we are led to believe the unbelievable—namely, that death can be avoided and life go on forever.

Everything in the universe exists *only* if it stands in contrast to something else. Stars exist because they are surrounded by the firmament. The heavens exist by virtue of the stars—the "breaks" in the heaven. "Day" without "night" is a meaningless concept. You can't have a high without a low, a back without a front, a winter without a summer. One phase defines another. When one disappears it is not the *other* that remains. One has, instead, amorphousness. So it is with death—one part of the cycle, the pulse, without which life is both meaningless and impossible. We arose out of death (nonlife) and will, of course, return to it. And out of that reservoir of nonlife, life must bloom again.

Besides which, no structure in the universe lasts "forever." Stars are "born" and "die." As do galaxies. As do the most minute atomic particles with their half-lives and no lives. To the sun, in its relative enormity, its life-span of billions of years is no longer or shorter than that of the katydid—whose time-span is measured in days. And yet, with all of these "deaths" (destruction of structure), the materials of which everything is created remain indestructible. Like the perfectly balanced ecological system. The blades of grass, the trees, the insects and wildlife "die" and are perpetually reborn. Forever and ever.

One big fear we have of death is that it represents *THE END*. Yet there is a psychotherapist I know, Ellen R., who, following surgery, "died" in the operating room. Her heart and breathing stopped for several minutes. She was aware of hearing the doctors and nurses say that she had expired, while at the same time feeling a tremendous "lightness" in her being. She wished that she could tell her friends that dying wasn't so bad and that she was still there, but she knew that she couldn't. She "heard" all the discussions in the operating room as they brought her back to life. Later, after recovering, she shared this "dream" with her physician only to find that he verified all the conversations she heard while she was both anesthetized and clinically dead.

We also fear *the end* because we tend to confuse ourselves with our *egos;* with our material surroundings. With our jobs, our clothes, our friends, our country, our names, our cars, our skins. If they disappear, then we do. Yet *there is no end* to be afraid of. Because the universe we know of is based not on *endings*, but *transformations*. When we drift off to sleep, for example, there is no precise point at which wakefulness ends and sleep begins. It is one subtle and continuous process (the same statement is true of conception). Yet the sleeper has no knowledge of the person who is awake. The sleeping *you* could not give your name, rank, and serial number. Nor could this *you* define your sex and age. The sleeping *you* is, rather, an observer. Recording scenes played out somewhere. In your mind's eye? In your cells? In some magical universe? It witnesses tragedies, nightmares, comedies, mysteries, adventures. Which is the real *you*? The sleeper or the waker?

Gurdjieff, the Russian philosopher/mystic, talked about the eternal you being the observer—the Witness. Detached from your body. Buddhists, Hindus, Taoists all describe the same real or eternal *you*. A you that has no connection with your body but observes and embraces all. The experience of this *you* is called cosmic consciousness, nirvana, samadhi, satori, enlightenment, revelation. It is the experience of realizing that you are not attached to your body and, instead, are linked inextricably with everything. That you are endless. That you had no beginning and will have no end.

Even from a scientifically oriented Western point of view you will, indeed, live forever. For your ego will never record its own death. We know, for instance, that there is a time lag between an event and our recording of it. Something occurs. We stub our toe. A certain time elapses during which the nervous tissue sends a message to our brain. A split second later we feel it. And in another fragment of a second we howl. We function much like cameras. A picture is taken, the film is developed, and the print is then seen and appreciated. So it is that you can never see and feel your own death (by *you* I don't mean the *detached you*, but the ego that you think of as *you*). The final snapshot is never developed for witnessing. Thus your ego is left fearing an event that will never befall it.

Another fear regarding death is the fear of the unknown. Those people who have the greatest difficulty accepting death frequently live rigid and stereotypical lives. Everything in order. No surprises. Novelty upsets them and they are not at peace until they can reestablish their usual routines and interpret new events along the lines of their habitual concepts.

Death, of course, is the greatest unknown. No one has ever come back to tell us what it was like. Or if they have (by being revived after being pronounced clinically dead—or through spiritual contact), most of our established "thinkers" set out to prove that it wasn't real. After all, we are told, if the person was revived he wasn't truly dead. Ipso facto, the "thinker" has proved his prejudgment—that the "dead" cannot go on living. This same disproval process happens with people who have reported contact with spirits—witness the case of Bishop James Pike.

So we are left with death as The Big Unknown. People

who have learned to live fully—who have come to appreciate the rush of excitement that comes on entering a totally unknown situation—have less trouble accepting death. For them it is the challenge of another unknown. They have learned to interpret excitement as *adventure* instead of *fear*.

Undergoing great pain and suffering is yet another thing people fear when they think of dying. We have heard about or witnessed the screams and suffering of dying people. My father died of cancer after an illness that lasted for over four years. He, in turn, had seen his father die of that same disease. He often told me that his one hope was that he would not suffer *his* father's pain, for he had witnessed the old gentleman bravely "waste away to a skeleton" before the end came.

My dad, of course, did have bouts of pain. But they were quite endurable. The day before he died he was still expressing the hope that he *wouldn't* go through the suffering and wasting process that his father had. Yet at that time he himself was so thin that he resembled a Nazi concentration camp victim.

I was with my father the night that he died. Sitting and holding his hand. Watching the pained faces he made. Hearing his periodic screams. Yet he told me, between death seizures, that he felt very peaceful. These experiences made me realize that those watching a man die often interpret more pain than the dying person experiences. Like watching women in labor. To an outsider it seems dreadful. The mother, however, is usually more impressed with the excitement of the experience. The pain that my father endured may have been no different than that. Or the pain that the fetus undergoes as it "dies" and is—in that same process—born.

The American Cancer Society, in its attempts to raise funds, has conditioned us to believe that cancer is the greatest scourge of all. But having shared my father's dying with him, I came to realize that cancer is a far better way to go than most people realize. For you have time to prepare yourself and your family for the transition. And you can witness your own "fading away" more leisurely and with greater awareness than you could from dying in your sleep, suffering a heart attack, or being hit by a truck.

There is more to death than overcoming your fear of it, however. For if you are willing to realize, each day, that you and those close to you might not be around in your current forms by the time tomorrow rolls around, *your life will take on an immediacy* and a *fulfillment* that it might otherwise be lacking.

You wouldn't postpone important things for the tomorrows that never dawn. You wouldn't wait "for a more convenient time" to resolve your differences with your parents, take your kids to that ball game you're always promising to take them to, or tell those closest to you how much you love them. You would, instead, drink fully from the cup of life each and every day. You would make every moment count.

Death is, then, something not to be "pushed out of mind" when it occurs to you but, instead, thought about, savored, and meditated upon. People who try to suppress such thoughts are misguided fools—and are often repaid by obsessional thoughts of death that hound them *simply because these thoughts are not thought through*. Letting yourself go with these thoughts will not only better prepare you for your own eventual journey into death but enable you to appreciate and reap a fuller harvest from life.

EXERCISES

1. Pretend that you have been told by your physician that you have only one month to live. Fantasize how you will spend

your remaining time. Whom will you see? What will you do? Where will you go?

2. Write a short composition explaining why you are not now doing all those things you would do if you had only one month to live.

3. Write your own obituary as it would be likely to appear if you died today. Include in it your accomplishments, your "essences," and whom you left behind.

4. Write another obituary as it would appear if you died in your old age. Make this an "ideal" obituary—as you would like things to read.

5. Consider how fully you are striving in life to make the obituary of exercise 3 read like that in exercise 4.

6. For the next week, live each day as if there will be no tomorrow. Upon arising and after each meal, tell yourself that this is your last day. Do and experience those things you would most like to do and experience before you die. Complete unspoken and unfinished things with other people.

7. Talk to several of your friends about dying—share your thoughts/fears/expectations and get them to do the same.

8. If it is at all possible, spend time with a dying person. Don't discuss the weather but, instead, share feelings about death.

17

CONCLUSION

IT is time for concluding; for recapitulation, wrapping up, and indicating other directions of personal growth that go beyond mental health.

The work you have undertaken has been based upon two key premises. These are the striving toward complete openness and honesty with others regarding all aspects of your life (feelings, thoughts, and actions) and acting counterphobically (entering into unknown situations—acting against, challenging and exploring your fears). These are the basic ingredients underlying all forms of successful psychotherapy.

Part of my nature (and so, I assume, part of yours) has been to start new projects with a great deal of excitement. After the initial enthusiasm wears off, it requires a concentrated effort to see the task through. If I don't make that secondary commitment, the work remains incomplete and the lessons I have learned from it remain amorphous and unclear.

It is my firm conviction that *this book will work for you if you see it through.*

You may have made only a partial commitment to some of the exercises along the way. Perhaps you ought, at this time, to return to them and see them through. You may well want to reread and reexperience exercises in those chapters covering areas you still have difficulty dealing with. You are certainly not the same person now that you were when you began. For life offers a continuously changing flow which has to have its own influence upon you. As the Buddhist saying puts it: You never stand in the same stream twice. In the same way, returning to certain chapters and exercises can be a *new* as well as useful experience.

Perhaps you rushed through this book. If so, repeat the work more leisurely. As I mentioned in my opening chapter, one should spend a week or two on each chapter before moving on. Using that time schedule, it should take you anywhere from four to eight months to complete *Do-It-Yourself-Psychotherapy*. Lessons have to sink in, be absorbed, and practiced in order to be mastered. This process requires time, persistence, and patience.

People in formal psychotherapy often return, months or years later, to clear up new confusions. The same procedure may be of use in self-therapy. Keep this book on your shelf and refer back to it when needed. Or open it arbitrarily in six months' to a year's time to see if you are still honestly taking care of business.

Each of the preceding chapters has dealt with some important aspect of living where troubles are likely to arise. The one area I have left out has been that of living with someone as a couple. This has been intentional and with good reason.

In this *self*-therapy book, the assumption always has been that you take responsibility for yourself and work on yourself —not on somebody else or on an intangible "relationship." Taking responsibility means that when you are angry at someone you don't say "*You* make me angry," but instead, "*I* get angry when you do such and such a thing." It is then up to you to examine the causes of your anger and not try to lay the responsibility for it on someone else's shoulders.

Living successfully as a couple requires, I believe, a great deal of luck and good fortune. It assumes that you and your partner will continue to grow along the same lines so that you share as many interests in the present (and will continue to do so in some *future* present) as you shared when you first met. Either that, or you are prepared to truly accept differing interests and doing more and more things apart from one another.

Couples run into trouble when their interests begin to differ and one or the other member of the pair has difficulty in accepting this. Manipulations, cajoling, blame, frustration, and resentments ensue. Often an amicable separation leaves both parties freer, more fulfilled, and able to seek a greater mutuality of interests with someone else. To remain together—with neither partner willing to compromise interests and aims that are growing apart *and* causing tensions—is the hellhole that so many couples find themselves in.

I believe that if you have worked properly on *yourself*, have gotten out of the *blaming game*, and have begun to honestly say what you feel, think, and desire, you are in the best position possible to make *one half* of a couple. To have the surest chance of making a couple relationship work requires that you pair up with someone *who also* operates under the same set of principles. If you are living with someone who doesn't accept these same ground rules, who is dishonest, who does a lot of blaming, whose responses are ambiguous and vague, who never lets you know where he or she stands, then all the books and all the advice in the world will not make for a fulfilling relationship.

So we are back to the basics—working on *self* instead of others as the best guarantee of forming decent relationships with others.

There are also several books I should like to recommend

to you, depending on your interests. All of them have had a special influence upon my own thinking.

If the "reasoning" approach to overcoming troublesome emotional feelings appeals to you (Albert Ellis' A-B-C approach—see chapter 5), I would recommend his book *Reason and Emotion in Psychotherapy* (Lyle Stuart, publisher). If you want more practice living in the *here* and *now* and/or found the Gestalt exercises helpful (those exercises where you worked with empty chairs and playacted at being those people you were annoyed at or fearful of), I refer you to *Gestalt Therapy Verbatim* by Frederick Perls and *Awareness* by John Stevens (both books are published by Real People Press).

Bernard Gunther's *Sense Relaxation* (Collier Books) presents the reader with numerous touching/feeling/massaging exercises for those of you who want to do more body work. *Yoga Self-Taught* by André Van Lysebeth (Harper & Row) is a clear and lucid instructional book on this subject that will, if pursued, not only help you achieve the sound body that a sound mind requires, but should also promote an inner tranquillity.

Two autobiographies of people attempting to live unashamedly in the *here* and *now* are Frederick Perls's *In and Out of the Garbage Pail* (Real People Press) and my own *A Psychiatrist's Head* (published by Peter H. Wyden). Both give a much fuller description of the implications and expectations of living in the present than could a single chapter in this book.

The Psychedelic Experience by Metzner, Leary, and Alpert (University Books) is an extremely useful book for anyone who has used or contemplates using psychedelic drugs. It is a guide book, based upon the *Tibetan Book of the Dead,* that is intended to help the psychedelic traveler enter into the religious experience and overcome the fear of dying.

The Wisdom of Lao-Tse (Modern Library) is an especially good volume which expands upon accepting life as it is and "going with the flow"—both tenets of Taoism. *Psychotherapy East and West* by Alan Watts (Ballantine Books) relates psychotherapy to these same Eastern disciplines.

Finally there is *Be Here Now*, put out by the Lama Foundation and distributed by Crown Publishing. This is the most impressive book I have read in the past several years. It contains the story of Richard Alpert's* transformation into Baba Ram Dass, useful meditative passages, and a collection of both ancient and contemporary wisdom which can readily be put to use in one's own life.

The question remains, though, "Where does one go after learning to like oneself—after learning to feel secure and comfortable?" The answer lies in examining the world beyond mental health.

Man's three areas of relationship are (1) to himself, (2) to other men, and (3) to his environment. *Do-It-Yourself Psychotherapy* has focused on only one aspect of one of these relationships. It offers a way out of man's mistrust of himself, man's lack of confidence in himself, and man's failure to grasp those satisfactions that life offers up to him. All of these things are subsumed under the first category—man's relationship to himself—and cover what is referred to as "mental health."

There are aspects of this same category that transcend mental health, however. These include the development of standards of ethics, goals, and spiritual values. Also included are commitments to knowledge, truth, understanding, and love.

---

* Richard Alpert, Ph.D., was, along with Dr. Timothy Leary, one of this country's first LSD researchers. After studying Ashtanga Yoga, in India, he returned here as Baba Ram Dass.

The *Be Here Now* book serves as an excellent introduction to these spheres of relating-to-self.

If this planet is to offer greater fulfillment to its inhabitants, however, it is imperative that each and every one of us pay attention to and make commitments toward working on the second two categories.

When men's relationships with their fellows are based upon exploitation, the exploiters suffer as much as those they are exploiting. For they are weakened by the inner decay produced by the imposition of unfair practices upon others. They must also maintain a perpetual suspiciousness and paranoia against their fellows, lest someone treat them as poorly as they treat others and to forestall an uprising and retaliation by those they exploit. Such practices have resulted in our contemporary world of "haves" and "have nots," of wars between Irish Catholics and Protestants, Arabs and Jews, Pakistanis and Bangladeshians, Vietnamese and Americans. It results in violence here at home between convicts and prison guards, blacks and whites, and assaults from the militants on both the right and left wings.

We, living in America, who consume more of the world's resources than any other people on the earth, whose high, industrial standard of living is based upon poor agrarian countries supplying us with cheap raw materials and labor, have a special obligation to "right the score." To not do so only fosters internal decay and the likelihood of violence when those who are downtrodden decide to take our wealth from us.

It is, finally, necessary to examine and slow down the destruction we are bringing to our planet if we and our children are to live healthy and full lives. Our air is befouled, our waters polluted, our countryside ravaged by billboards, strip mining, garbage, and parking lots.

Our food is sprayed, while it is growing, with dangerous chemicals, packaged with dangerous preservatives, colored with dangerous dyes. We consume and consume and consume and consume. We blame the government for not clearing up the waste products of our own consumption and at the same time are unwilling to pay the higher taxes required and unwilling to cut down on our demandingness for new goods. As a society we seem more concerned with the Gross National Product than with the quality of our lives.

It isn't Con Edison's fault if New Yorkers have polluted air and electrical breakdowns. It is the fault, instead, of every New Yorker who insists on air conditioning in his home and office, electric brooms, electric can openers, electric blenders, electric clocks, etc. etc. etc. Such insistent consumption— whatever its immediate rewards—creates the smog produced by generating so much electricity. The same environmental problems are produced by our insistence on owning auto-mobiles, having throwaway bottles and cans, having "whiter than white" washing compounds, and our tendency to throw out, rather than salvage, old equipment.

To fully live one's life, then, requires that we not only learn to live with ourselves (the purpose of this book) but learn to live with our fellows and more simply within our environ-ment. We can't afford to live in conflict with either. Conquer-ing other men or conquering nature is as foolhardy an idea as attempts to conquer oneself would be. We must, instead, strive to live out and express our own natural selves while living *naturally* with our fellows and *within* the confines of nature.

18

RULES

The following list is a brief restatement of those mental health principles elaborated upon in this book:

1. Learn to interpret your anxiety as excitement instead of nervousness.

2. Don't do anything you can't share, and be prepared to discuss everything that you do.

3. Expect nothing and you will have no one and nothing to blame.

4. Assume that everything that happens to you is your own doing.

5. If you are truly yourself, you will eventually find people who love and respect you.

6. When you are dissatisfied, ask yourself what it is that you really feel like doing right now—and try to do it.

7. It is better to ask for what you want and get a "No," than never ask and ensure no gratification.

8. Touch people more often.

9. People are responsible for their own orgasms.

10. Whenever you feel in conflict with someone, play out both sides and become the person you are angry at.

11. Remember—grown-ups are merely children in aging skin.

12. Destroy your concept of normality. The only person who can go crazy is one who has a preconception of what sanity is.

13. One way to go beyond your present act is to explore roles you are reluctant to play.

14. Listening to people can be as stimulating and intelligent an act as talking to them.

15. You don't need a friend along to do those things you want to do.

16. A meaningful job is essential for emotional well-being.

17. Treat others in the way you wish them to treat you.

18. To get people to confide in you, you must first confide in them.

19. Always remember to say what you feel.

20. Meditate on death daily to give your life more meaning.